—Real Food—
Gluten-free
Bread & Cakes
from your Breadmaker

— Real Food —
Gluten-free
Bread & Cakes
from your Breadmaker

Carolyn Humphries

foulsham
LONDON • NEW YORK • TORONTO • SYDNEY

foulsham

The Publishing House, Bennetts Close, Cippenham,
Slough, Berkshire, SL1 5AP, England

ISBN 0-572-03002-9

Copyright © 2004 W. Foulsham & Co. Ltd

Cover photograph © Cephas/Stock Food

Illustrations by Jane Norman

A CIP record for this book is available from the British Library

With thanks to Morphy Richards and Panasonic for the loan of
breadmakers used in the testing of these recipes.

Other books by Foulsham:
Your Wheat-free Gluten-free Diet Plan, Carolyn Humphries,
0-572-02672-2
Your Allergy-free Diet Plan for Babies and Children, Carolyn
Humphries, 0-572-02891-1

Printed in Great Britain by Mackays of Chatham plc, Chatham, Kent

Contents

Real Gluten-free Breads

'These loaves all behave like "real" bread. They slice perfectly – no crumbly messes – and they toast properly so can be used straight from the freezer for breakfast. Because they're larger than any you can buy they're great for sandwiches.'

'The Milk Loaf is the nearest thing I've had to a proper white loaf since I've been on a wheat-free diet. It smells and tastes delicious and the texture is exceptional.'

If you are on a gluten-free diet, those quotes from people who have eaten the loaves I made while working on this book are likely to be music to your ears. Just imagine eating a simple slice of bread and butter – light, soft and deliciously doughy! It's probably what you've missed most since going on to a gluten-free diet – and now you can enjoy it again as often as you like.

Almost certainly you already know that just about every ordinary bread or cake contains gluten, which is the protein in wheat and some other grains that makes doughs airy and light and gives bread that lovely elastic quality. Without it, they are just not the same – until now.

Of course, there are lots of specialist baked goods available in supermarkets and health food shops but they are expensive and can often be rather disappointing. The tendency is for them to be small, dense and too chewy. You can also make gluten-free loaves without a breadmaker, but that can be time-consuming and the results may not be quite as good as you'd like because you don't always have exactly the right conditions to prove the loaves in the kitchen – it may have been too hot, too cold, too draughty or too humid.

Using a breadmaker eliminates all the effort *and* the imponderables so you end up with perfect results every time. The only things you really must do are measure everything accurately, as small errors can cause big disasters, and always put the ingredients into the pan in the order listed. How simple is that?

All the recipes in this book have been rigorously tested to guarantee good results. You can create a whole repertoire of breads, from simply delicious white and brown loaves – probably the ones you'll use all the time – to such mouth-watering delights as a focaccia – made with olive oil and studded with sun-dried tomatoes, olives and fragrant fresh basil – or heavenly, flaky all-butter croissants. You can use your breadmaker to bake cakes too (cheaper than using the oven!) so I've included a selection for you to try. Plus there's a range of moist tea breads, breadsticks, pizzas, bagels, muffins and even hot-cross buns!

The recipes in this book were tested using a Morphy Richards Fastbake and a Panasonic SD-253. The Panasonic breadmaker has a gluten-free setting, which is fine for using commercial gluten-free bread mixes, but I used the 'normal' settings for my recipes so you can make them whatever breadmaker you have.

Getting Used to Gluten-free Baking

If you've ever made your own bread by hand, you'll know that it is not always the simplest job: yeast can be temperamental; you can run out of energy and not knead the dough for long enough; the temperature of the air and of the ingredients can affect the outcome, as can the proportion of liquid. Using a breadmaker, of course, helps take away some of these variables and makes the whole thing a lot easier.

But if you need to make gluten-free bread you have a whole new set of problems. Gluten-free flours are weirder than most. They don't stretch on their own, some of them can taste *unusual* (and that's putting a positive slant on it!) and some don't even brown in the same way as wheat flour. They need more yeast than the average wheat loaf and, for the most part, bread mixes have to be the consistency of a thick batter rather than a pliable dough.

All that may sound complicated, but you don't need to worry. In the first place, these softer doughs are more thoroughly kneaded in a breadmaker than by hand. In the second, I've done loads of experimentation over a number of years to find ways round these problems to create recipes that are as foolproof as humanly possible.

My range of mouth-watering breads and cakes uses combinations of gluten-free flours and flour mixes available in supermarkets, often with the addition of xanthum gum (sometimes called xanthan) which, added to the flour, gives it an elasticity similar to that of gluten. I've used a myriad of additional ingredients to give you fabulous flavours and textures you'll really enjoy for every meal of the day. But, probably best of all, now when you just want a slice of bread and butter – you can. Even the basic white and brown loaves taste so good – especially when still warm straight from the breadmaker – that they don't need a giant spoonful of strong-flavoured conserve or a savoury spread to make them palatable.

Gluten-free Baking in Your Breadmaker

There are now a vast number of breadmakers on the market, all with different settings, timings and electronic idiosyncrasies – and competing in a price war to boot! Suffice to say they all do a similar job, albeit with different timings. Times can vary considerably so you should check your manufacturer's instructions.

In order to ensure that the breads in my book can be made in any breadmaker, I've made them using only the Basic, Dough or Bake-only settings. That way, even if you have one of the simpler machines, you will still be able to make the breads as you don't need any of the sophisticated settings available on the more expensive models. Even though different machines have slightly different timings and settings, they will all produce similar results on the programmes I've used.

Some machines have a cake setting but, as they don't all, I've mixed the ingredients for cakes, then used the breadmaker as an oven – which uses far less fuel than a conventional one. Obviously, if yours has a cake setting, experiment with my recipes following the manufacturer's instructions.

Your machine may rest and warm the ingredients before it actually starts the baking process. I have not allowed for this in any timings in the book. However if, for instance, I am using a dough programme but not letting the dough prove in the machine, I have said it's usually about 20 minutes in the machine. This is from the time the machine starts mixing the ingredients until it stops to start warming up.

Flour Mixes

For many of the recipes in this book, you can buy commercially prepared plain white and brown gluten-free flour mixes or you can make your own using the recipes on page 12. These mixes can be used for bread and cakes. You'll see in the recipes that for most breads you need to add xanthum gum (the quantities are given in each recipe) to give them the added elasticity needed to make them rise well and have a springy, open, bubbly texture.

Converting Standard Bread Recipes

If you want to experiment with your own bread recipes, you can turn these flour mixes into flours similar to ordinary wheat bread flours by adding 5 ml/1 tsp xanthum gum for every 100 g/4 oz/ 1 cup of gluten-free flour mix. You can use commercially prepared gluten-free bread flour mixes but I find they make very gluey loaves. However, if you don't have xanthum gum, I've found that you can use half commercial gluten-free bread flour mix and half of one of the gluten-free plain flour mixes. As I said before, using all gluten-free bread flour doesn't give good results in my recipes.

Store the home-made flour mixes as you would ordinary flour.

If you are converting your wheat bread recipes to gluten-free ones, you will obviously have to replace all the wheat flours with gluten-free alternatives. You will need to add more liquid too – the consistency for most (except pizza and the shaped ones) needs to be like a thick batter, not a pliable dough.

White gluten-free flour mix

MAKES 650 G/1½ LB/6 CUPS

50 g/2 oz/½ cup tapioca flour or buckwheat flour
50 g/2 oz/½ cup cornflour (cornstarch)
100 g/4 oz/1 cup potato flour
450 g/1 lb/4 cups white rice flour

1 Mix all the ingredients together and store in a covered container.

2 Use as required.

Brown gluten-free flour mix

If you like a higher fibre mix, add 50 g/ 2 oz/½ cup rice bran to the mixture. When converting your own recipes to use gluten-free brown flour, try using black treacle instead of some or all of the sugar in the recipe too.

MAKES 650 G/1½ LB/6 CUPS

50 g/2 oz/½ cup buckwheat flour
50 g/2 oz/½ cup tapioca or quinoa flour
100 g/4 oz/1 cup potato flour
450 g/1 lb/4 cups brown rice flour
15 ml/1 tbsp gluten-free cocoa powder

1 Mix all the ingredients together and store in a covered container.

2 Use as required.

Notes on Gluten-free Breadmaking Recipes

○ Always put the wet ingredients in the pan before the dry ones and always keep the yeast separate from the liquid, so add it last on top of the flours. The ingredients are listed in the order they should be added to the pan, which makes the recipes very easy to follow.

○ Measure ingredients exactly, using the measuring spoons and cup supplied with your breadmaker – never use ordinary teaspoons or tablespoons. You may weigh the flours on your scales, if that's easier, but be accurate! Spoon measures are always level.

○ All the ingredients are given in metric, imperial and American measures. Use only one set per recipe, never a combination.

○ American terms for ingredients and utensils are given in brackets.

○ Fill the pan outside the breadmaker to avoid dropping any ingredients on the element in the machine. Then place the pan in position and make sure it has clicked into place.

○ If you like softer, paler loaves, go for the lighter crust settings. I often use dark because I find some gluten-free flours don't brown quite as well as wheat ones and I like a rich brown crust. Experiment for yourselves.

○ If you leave the bread in the breadmaker for up to 1 hour before removing it, the crust will soften. I usually suggest leaving the cooked loaf for 10 minutes as this often prevents the paddle getting stuck in the loaf. However, you can turn them out immediately if you prefer.

o Don't use the timer settings. Gluten-free mixes don't work well after sitting for hours.

o Always check the ingredients a couple of minutes after mixing starts and scrape down the sides, if necessary, with a plastic (never metal) spatula to prevent a build-up of flour around the edges, taking care not to touch the rotating paddle.

o If your machine doesn't have a viewing window (which is extremely useful), once you've scraped down the sides and know the mixture is the right sort of consistency, don't be tempted to peep again unless it's to add ingredients as specified in a recipe. If you keep doing so during the heating, rising or baking process, you could ruin your loaf.

o When the programme is complete, always use oven gloves to lift the pan out of the machine as the pan and the machine will be very hot.

o Always wipe down the machine inside and outside after use and never use any abrasive materials or cleaner on any part of it. Wash the pan and paddle with warm, soapy water and dry well.

o Eggs are medium unless otherwise stated.

o For some recipes I've used easy-blend fast-acting yeast: for others the ordinary active dried yeast (that you usually mix with liquid and sugar first but not when using it in the breadmaker) is best. The reason is that for some recipes the easy-blend variety works too quickly. For best results do as I have done, but if you don't have both varieties, use easy-blend for all recipes. Do not use fresh yeast.

o Always wrap flavoured loaves before storing.

Solving Problems

In any kind of cooking there's no substitute for experience and breadmaking is no exception. You'll soon get used to your own machine, the sort of consistency you're looking for in your doughs and even the right conditions in your kitchen, to help you get the best results.

As I said at the beginning, in gluten-free baking you do need to measure your ingredients carefully and put them into the breadmaker pan in the order specified. If you do that, you should be fine; if your loaf didn't turn out quite as expected, it could just mean you need to be a little more precise next time. Alternatively, if you're experimenting with your own recipes, you'll need to know how to rectify common problems.

Here are a few troubleshooting hints:

Problem	Solutions
The surface of the finished loaf is cracked and isn't brown.	The mixture was too wet; add a little less liquid next time.
The surface of the loaf is damp and sticky.	The bread was left in the breadmaker too long and condensation has formed; remove it from the machine 10 minutes after the programme ends next time. OR the mixture was too wet; reduce the liquid slightly next time.
The loaf rose beautifully but collapsed when cooked.	The mixture may have been too wet; reduce the liquid slightly next time. OR you may have added too much yeast; reduce by 1.5 ml/¼ tsp. OR there may not be enough salt; increase by 1.5 ml/¼ tsp. OR you may have opened the lid during baking. Don't!
The loaf is dry and crumbly.	The mixture was too dry; add a little more liquid next time.

Problem	Solutions
The loaf didn't rise enough.	There wasn't enough yeast; increase by 1.5 ml/¼ tsp next time. OR there was too little sugar; increase by 1.5 ml/¼ tsp. OR there was too much salt, which kills the yeast; decrease by 1.5 ml/¼ tsp. OR the yeast was in contact with the liquid so was already activated before the programme started; keep the yeast and liquid separate. OR the yeast is too old; throw it out and buy a new packet.
The bread rose too much and the finished loaf has a large holey texture.	The mixture was too wet; reduce the liquid slightly next time. OR there was too much yeast; reduce by 1.5 ml/¼ tsp. OR the liquid was too hot; the liquid should usually be cold or, occasionally, warm – never hot. OR there wasn't enough salt so the yeast was over-active; increase by 1.5 ml/¼ tsp.
The texture is sticky.	The mixture was too wet; reduce the liquid slightly next time. OR the loaf didn't cook for long enough; extend the cooking time using the bake programme or set the breadmaker to a large loaf size.
The loaf is too brown.	There was too much sugar; reduce by 1.5 ml/¼ tsp next time. OR the crust-colour setting was too high for that loaf; reduce it next time.
The loaf isn't brown on top.	The crust setting was too low; increase it next time. OR There wasn't enough mixture in the pan for the top to brown; make the right quantity for the pan size next time. OR there was too little sugar; add an extra 1.5 ml/¼ tsp.

Problem	Solutions
The bread sticks to the pan.	Your pan wasn't cleaned after the last loaf.
	OR you tried to take the loaf out of the machine too soon; leave it in the breadmaker for 10 minutes before turning out (this also helps prevent the paddle from staying inside the loaf).
	OR the pan needs 'seasoning'. Wash it well in warm, soapy water, rinse and dry, then brush liberally all over the inside with oil. Place it in the machine, select the bake programme and heat the empty pan for 10 minutes. Wipe it out thoroughly with kitchen paper (paper towels) or wash and dry again.

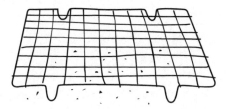

Basic Breads

These are recipes for good loaves for everyday eating. They vary in texture and flavour but all are terrific alternatives to wheat breads. They all slice well –even thinly – so are ideal for sandwiches as well as toast or as doorsteps!

You will see that some are best with easy-blend dried yeast, others with ordinary active dried yeast. Either way, you don't need to 'activate' it first but can use it dry.

You can use a mix from page 12 or bought gluten-free plain flour in the recipes. Don't use bought gluten-free bread flour though, unless particularly stated, as the results will be very gluey!

Everyday white bread

This is a good all-purpose loaf that's very versatile and great for everything, from toast to sandwiches. It's robust enough to stand being topped with baked beans or other saucy toppings.

MAKES 1 MEDIUM LOAF

1 egg

350 ml/12 fl oz/1⅓ cups water

60 ml/4 tbsp sunflower oil

5 ml/1 tsp lemon juice

7.5 ml/1½ tsp salt

20 ml/1½ tbsp caster (superfine) sugar

400 g/14 oz/3½ cups white gluten-free flour mix (see pages 11 and 12)

15 ml/1 tbsp xanthum gum

15 ml/1 tbsp active dried yeast

1 Beat together the egg and water, then pour into the breadmaker pan.

2 Add all the remaining ingredients in the order listed.

3 Set the machine to Basic, 700 g/1½ lb/Medium, dark crust.

4 When cooked, switch off the machine and leave the bread to cool in the breadmaker for 10 minutes.

5 Turn the bread out of the pan on to a wire rack. When cool enough to handle, remove the paddle, if necessary.

6 When cold, store in the bread bin for up to four days or slice and freeze.

Milk loaf

*You'll have to be around when this one is cooking because
it doesn't need the full pre-set cooking time. It's worth the
hanging around though because the flavour and texture
are fantastic!*

MAKES 1 MEDIUM LOAF

1 large egg

275 ml/9 fl oz/scant 1¼ cups
  milk

15 ml/1 tbsp sunflower oil

4 ml/¾ tsp salt

15 ml/1 tbsp caster (superfine)
  sugar

225 g/8 oz/2 cups white rice
  flour

10 ml/2 tsp xanthum gum

1 sachet of easy-blend dried yeast

1 Beat together the egg and milk, then pour into the
    breadmaker pan.

2 Add all the remaining ingredients in the order listed.

3 Set the machine to Basic, 700 g/1½ lb/Medium, dark
    crust but allow to cook for 40 minutes only or until
    golden and firm to the touch and shrinking slightly from
    the sides of the pan.

4 When cooked, switch off the machine and leave the
    bread to cool in the breadmaker for 10 minutes.

5 Turn the bread out of the pan on to a wire rack. When
    cool enough to handle, remove the paddle, if necessary.

6 When cold, store in the bread bin for up to four days or
    slice and freeze.

Buttermilk bread

*This one has a slightly coarser texture than the
Milk Loaf on page 21. It makes a nice change though
and is a tasty, nutritious choice,
especially good toasted.*

MAKES 1 MEDIUM LOAF

3 eggs

284 ml/9 fl oz/1 carton of
buttermilk

75 ml/5 tbsp milk

10 ml/2 tsp lemon juice

20 ml/1½ tbsp golden (light
corn) syrup

45 ml/3 tbsp sunflower oil

7.5 ml/1½ tsp salt

225 g/8 oz/2 cups white rice
flour

25 g/1 oz/¼ cup cornflour
(cornstarch)

50 g/2 oz/½ cup soya flour

50 g/2 oz/½ cup potato flour

15 ml/1 tbsp xanthum gum

15 ml/1 tbsp active dried yeast

1 Beat together the eggs, buttermilk and milk, then pour
   into the breadmaker pan.

2 Add the lemon juice, syrup, oil and salt.

3 Mix together the flours and gum and add to the pan.
   Top with the yeast.

4 Set the machine to Basic, 700 g/1½ lb/Medium, light or
   medium crust.

5 When cooked, switch off the machine and leave the
   bread to cool in the breadmaker for 10 minutes.

6 Turn the bread out of the pan on to a wire rack. When
   cool enough to handle, remove the paddle, if necessary.

7 When cold, store in the bread bin for up to four days or
   slice and freeze.

Basic brown bread

If you prefer the flavour and colour of brown loaves, then this delicious option will be your everyday favourite. It's just as versatile for everything from sandwiches to toast.

MAKES 1 MEDIUM LOAF

1 large egg

400 ml/14 fl oz/1³/₄ cups water

45 ml/3 tbsp dried milk powder (non-fat dry milk)

5 ml/1 tsp lemon juice

45 ml/3 tbsp sunflower oil

20 ml/1¹/₂ tbsp black treacle (molasses)

350 g/12 oz/3 cups brown rice flour

15 ml/1 tbsp xanthum gum

7.5 ml/1¹/₂ tsp salt

15 ml/1 tbsp active dried yeast

1 Beat together the egg, water and milk powder, then pour into the breadmaker pan.

2 Add the lemon juice, oil and treacle.

3 Top with the flour, gum and salt.

4 Finally, sprinkle the yeast on top.

5 Set the machine to Basic, 700 g/1¹/₂ lb/Medium, dark crust.

6 When cooked, switch off the machine and leave the bread to cool in the breadmaker for 10 minutes.

7 Turn the bread out of the pan on to a wire rack. When cool enough to handle, remove the paddle, if necessary.

8 When cold, store in the bread bin for up to four days or slice and freeze.

Moist brown loaf

Don't worry if this loaf sinks slightly as it won't alter its delicious moistness. If you do want to avoid this happening, you can cook the loaf for an extra 10–15 minutes but the texture will, of course, be drier.

MAKES 1 MEDIUM LOAF

2 eggs

375 ml/13 fl oz/1½ cups water

5 ml/1 tsp cider vinegar

45 ml/3 tbsp sunflower oil

15 ml/1 tbsp clear honey

15 ml/1 tbsp black treacle (molasses)

7.5 ml/1½ tsp salt

75 g/3 oz/¾ cup tapioca flour

50 g/2 oz/½ cup soya flour

225 g/8 oz/2 cups brown rice flour, plus extra for dusting

15 ml/1 tbsp xanthum gum

15 ml/1 tbsp active dried yeast

1 Beat together the eggs and water, then pour into the breadmaker pan.

2 Add the vinegar, oil, honey, treacle and salt.

3 Mix together the flours and gum and add to the pan. Sprinkle the yeast on top.

4 Set the machine to Basic, 700 g/1½ lb/Medium, dark crust.

5 When cooked, switch off the machine and leave the bread to cool in the breadmaker for 10 minutes.

6 Turn the bread out of the pan on to a wire rack. When cool enough to handle, remove the paddle, if necessary. Dust the surface with a little brown rice flour.

7 When cold, store in the bread bin for up to four days or slice and freeze.

Linseed brown loaf

Quinoa flour is available in healthfood shops and by mail order but if you don't have it to hand, just substitute more buckwheat or brown rice flour to make up the quantity.

MAKES 1 MEDIUM LOAF

1 large egg

350 ml/12 fl oz/1⅓ cups water

45 ml/3 tbsp dried milk powder (non-fat dry milk)

5 ml/1 tsp lemon juice

45 ml/3 tbsp sunflower oil

15 ml/1 tbsp black treacle (molasses)

10 ml/2 tsp light brown sugar

225 g/8 oz/2 cups brown rice flour

50 g/2 oz/½ cup quinoa flour

50 g/2 oz/½ cup buckwheat flour

15 ml/1 tbsp xanthum gum

7.5 ml/1½ tsp salt

15 ml/1 tbsp linseed

15 ml/1 tbsp active dried yeast

1 Beat together the egg, water and milk powder, then pour into the breadmaker pan.

2 Add the lemon juice, oil, treacle and sugar.

3 Top with the flours, gum, salt and linseed.

4 Finally, sprinkle the yeast on top.

5 Set the machine to Basic, 700 g/1½ lb/Medium, dark crust.

6 When cooked, switch off the machine and leave the bread to cool in the breadmaker for 10 minutes.

7 Turn the bread out of the pan on to a wire rack. When cool enough to handle, remove the paddle, if necessary.

8 When cold, store in the bread bin for up to four days or slice and freeze.

Millet flake bread

This makes a delicious loaf with a nutty flavour.
You could experiment using other gluten-free flakes,
like quinoa or buckwheat, if you like
other flavours.

MAKES 1 LARGE LOAF

1 egg

2 egg whites

350 ml/12 fl oz/1⅓ cups water

50 g/2 oz/¼ cup butter or margarine, melted

5 ml/1 tsp lemon juice

15 ml/1 tbsp clear honey

7.5 ml/1½ tsp salt

400 g/14 oz/3½ cups white gluten-free flour mix (see pages 11 and 12)

50 g/2 oz/½ cup millet flakes, plus 15 ml/1 tbsp for sprinkling

11.5 ml/2¼ tsp active dried yeast

A little milk for glazing

1 Beat together the egg, egg whites and water, then pour into the breadmaker pan.

2 Add the melted butter or margarine, lemon juice, honey and salt.

3 Add the flour, millet flakes and yeast.

4 Set the machine to Basic, 900 g/2 lb/Large, dark crust.

5 1 hour before the end of the programme, open the lid as little as possible and sprinkle with the 15 ml/1 tbsp millet flakes, then gently close the lid.

6 When cooked, switch off the machine and leave the bread to cool in the breadmaker for 10 minutes.

7 If the paddle is still in the loaf, carefully invert the loaf on to a plate to catch any loose flakes and remove the paddle. Transfer the loaf to a wire rack to cool completely.

8 When cold, store in a bread bin for up to four days or slice and freeze.

White potato bread

This is a handy way to use up leftover boiled potato if you have some. Use 225 g/8 oz instead of cooking a potato specially to make the loaf.

MAKES 1 LARGE LOAF

1 unpeeled large potato, scrubbed and pricked with a fork

2 large eggs

275 ml/9 fl oz/scant 1¼ cups water

50 g/2 oz/¼ cup butter or margarine, melted

5 ml/1 tsp distilled white vinegar

30 ml/2 tbsp caster (superfine) sugar

225 g/8 oz/2 cups white rice flour

50 g/2 oz/½ cup tapioca flour

100 g/4 oz/1 cup potato flour

7.5 ml/1½ tsp salt

10 ml/2 tsp powdered gelatine

15 ml/1 tbsp xanthum gum

20 ml/1½ tbsp active dried yeast

1 Boil the whole potato for about 20 minutes or bake in the microwave for about 4 minutes until soft. Drain, if necessary. Rinse under cold water to cool, then peel off the skin. Mash very thoroughly until no lumps remain.

2 Beat together the eggs and water, then pour into the breadmaker pan. Add the melted butter or margarine, vinegar and sugar, then the mashed potato.

3 Mix together the flours, salt, gelatine and gum, then tip into the pan. Sprinkle the yeast on top.

4 Set the machine to Basic, 900 g/2 lb/Large, medium or dark crust.

5 When cooked, switch off the machine and leave the bread to cool in the breadmaker for 10 minutes.

6 Turn the bread out of the pan on to a wire rack. When cool enough to handle, remove the paddle, if necessary.

7 When cold, store in the bread bin for up to four days or slice and freeze.

Rice and soya bread

It's fun to experiment with different flours,
rather than always using a prepared flour mix.
When you're on a gluten-free diet, these ones
are usually to hand!

MAKES 1 LARGE LOAF

2 eggs

375 ml/13 fl oz/1½ cups water

50 g/2 oz/¼ cup butter or margarine, melted

5 ml/1 tsp distilled white vinegar

20 ml/1½ tbsp caster (superfine) sugar

10 ml/2 tsp salt

60 ml/4 tbsp dried milk powder (non-fat dry milk)

150 g/5 oz/1¼ cups brown rice flour

150 g/5 oz/1¼ cups white rice flour

50 g/2 oz/½ cup potato flour

100 g/4 oz/1 cup soya flour

15 ml/1 tbsp xanthum gum

20 ml/1½ tbsp active dried yeast

1 Beat together the eggs and water, then pour into the breadmaker pan.

2 Add the melted butter or margarine, the vinegar, sugar, salt and milk powder.

3 Mix together the flours and gum and add to the breadmaker.

4 Finally, sprinkle the yeast on top.

5 Set the machine to Basic, 900 g/2 lb/Large, medium crust.

6 When cooked, switch off the machine and leave the bread to cool in the breadmaker for 10 minutes.

7 Turn the bread out of the pan on to a wire rack. When cool enough to handle, remove the paddle, if necessary.

8 When cold, store in the bread bin for up to four days or slice and freeze.

Bran bread

*This makes a great loaf with a higher fibre content –
something that can be lacking in a gluten-free diet.
Always make sure you eat plenty of nuts
and seeds too.*

MAKES 1 MEDIUM LOAF

2 large eggs

375 ml/13 fl oz/1½ cups milk

5 ml/1 tsp lemon juice

7.5 ml/1½ tsp salt

15 ml/1 tbsp golden (light corn)
syrup

50 g/2 oz/¼ cup butter or
margarine, melted

175 g/6 oz/1½ cups white rice
flour

200 g/7 oz/1¾ cups brown rice
flour

25 g/1 oz/¼ cup rice bran

15 ml/1 tbsp xanthum gum

15 ml/1 tbsp active dried yeast

1   Beat together the eggs and milk, then pour into the
breadmaker pan.

2   Add the lemon juice, salt, syrup and melted butter or
margarine.

3   Mix together the flours, bran and gum, then tip into the
pan.

4   Finally, sprinkle the yeast on top.

5   Set the machine to Basic, 700 g/1½ lb/Medium, medium
or dark crust.

6   When cooked, switch off the machine and leave the
bread to cool in the breadmaker for 10 minutes.

7   Turn the bread out of the pan on to a wire rack. When
cool enough to handle, remove the paddle, if necessary.

8   When cold, store in the bread bin for up to four days or
slice and freeze.

Rice flake bread

This is a deliciously moist loaf made with rice flours and flakes. You can buy similar rice-flour breads in most large supermarkets, but you'd have to pay twice the price for half the texture and flavour!

MAKES 1 LARGE LOAF

2 eggs

375 ml/13 fl oz/1½ cups water

50 g/2 oz/¼ cup butter or margarine, melted

5 ml/1 tsp distilled white vinegar

20 ml/1½ tbsp light brown sugar

10 ml/2 tsp salt

60 ml/4 tbsp dried milk powder (non-fat dry milk)

175 g/6 oz/1½ cups brown rice flour

175 g/6 oz/1½ cups white rice flour

50 g/2 oz/½ cup potato flour

50 g/2 oz/1½ cup rice flakes

15 ml/1 tbsp xanthum gum

20 ml/1½ tbsp active dried yeast

1 Beat together the eggs and water, then pour into the breadmaker pan.

2 Add the melted butter or margarine, vinegar, sugar, salt and milk powder.

3 Mix together the flours, rice flakes and gum and add to the breadmaker.

4 Finally, sprinkle the yeast on top.

5 Set the machine to Basic, 900 g/2 lb/Large, medium crust.

6 When cooked, switch off the machine and leave the bread to cool in the breadmaker for 10 minutes.

7 Turn the bread out of the pan on to a wire rack. When cool enough to handle, remove the paddle, if necessary.

8 When cold, store in the bread bin for up to four days or slice and freeze.

Moist white bread

This makes a moist, light-textured white loaf that is perfect just served with a little butter. Don't worry if it sinks slightly in the centre after cooking as this will not affect your enjoyment of the flavour!

MAKES 1 LARGE LOAF

1 egg

350 ml/12 fl oz/1⅓ cups water

65 g/2½ oz/generous ¼ cup butter or margarine, melted

5 ml/1 tsp lemon juice

15 ml/1 tbsp clear honey

100 g/4 oz/1 cup tapioca flour

225 g/8 oz/2 cups white rice flour

50 g/2 oz/½ cup potato flour

50 g/2 oz/½ cup cornflour (cornstarch), plus extra for dusting

15 ml/1 tbsp xanthum gum

7.5 ml/1½ tsp powdered gelatine

7.5 ml/1½ tsp salt

15 ml/1 tbsp caster (superfine) sugar

60 ml/4 tbsp dried milk powder (non-fat dry milk)

15 ml/1 tbsp active dried yeast

1 Beat together the egg and water, then pour into the breadmaker pan.

2 Add 50 g/2 oz/¼ cup of the melted butter or margarine, the lemon juice and honey.

3 Mix together the flours, gum, gelatine, salt, sugar and milk powder and add to the breadmaker.

4 Finally, sprinkle the yeast on top.

5 Set the machine to Basic, 900 g/2 lb/Large, light or medium crust.

6 When cooked, leave in the breadmaker for 10 minutes, then turn the bread out on to a wire rack. Brush the crust all over with the remaining melted butter or margarine to give a softer crust. Leave until cool enough to handle, then remove the paddle, if necessary. Dust the top with a little cornflour.

7 When cold, store in the bread bin for up to four days or slice and freeze.

Mock rye bread

Don't worry if this loaf sinks slightly – it won't alter the delicious moist texture. It can be alleviated by cooking the loaf for an extra 10–15 minutes on top of the timed cooking but it will result in a slightly drier consistency.

MAKES 1 MEDIUM LOAF

2 eggs

350 ml/12 fl oz/1⅓ cups water

5 ml/1 tsp cider vinegar

45 ml/3 tbsp sunflower oil

15 ml/1 tbsp clear honey

15 ml/1 tbsp black treacle (molasses)

7.5 ml/1½ tsp salt

75 g/3 oz/¾ cup tapioca flour

50 g/2 oz/½ cup soya flour

225 g/8 oz/2 cups brown rice flour, plus extra for dusting

15 ml/1 tbsp xanthum gum

15 ml/1 tbsp caraway seeds

15 ml/1 tbsp active dried yeast

1 Beat together the eggs and water, then pour into the breadmaker pan.

2 Add the vinegar, oil, honey, treacle and salt.

3 Mix together the flours and gum and add to the pan.

4 Sprinkle on the caraway seeds, then top with the yeast.

5 Set the machine to Basic, 700 g/1½ lb/Medium, dark crust.

6 When cooked, switch off the machine and leave the bread to cool in the breadmaker for 10 minutes.

7 Turn the bread out of the pan on to a wire rack. When cool enough to handle, remove the paddle, if necessary. Dust the surface with a little rice flour.

8 When cold, store in the bread bin for up to four days or slice and freeze.

Muesli loaf

This loaf has a lovely texture – especially when fresh – but it sometimes sinks in the middle slightly. To rectify this you can reduce the milk by 25 ml/1 fl oz but, although it will look better, the texture won't be quite so good.

MAKES 1 MEDIUM LOAF

2 eggs

50 g/2 oz/¼ cup butter or margarine, melted

175 ml/6 fl oz/¾ cup milk

150 ml/¼ pt/⅔ cup plain yoghurt

30 ml/2 tbsp clear honey

275 g/10 oz/2½ cups white gluten-free flour mix (see pages 11 and 12)

15 ml/1 tbsp xanthum gum

7.5 ml/1½ tsp salt

5 ml/1 tsp bicarbonate of soda (baking soda)

75 g/3 oz/¾ cup gluten-free muesli

15 ml/1 tbsp active dried yeast

1 Beat together the eggs, melted butter or margarine, milk and yoghurt. Pour into the breadmaker pan and add the honey.

2 Sift the flour with the gum, salt and bicarbonate of soda. Tip into the pan and add the muesli.

3 Finally, sprinkle the yeast on top.

4 Set the machine to Basic, 700 g/1½ lb/Medium, dark crust.

5 When cooked, switch off the machine and leave the bread to cool in the breadmaker for 10 minutes.

6 Turn the bread out of the pan on to a wire rack. When cool enough to handle, remove the paddle, if necessary.

7 When cold, store in the bread bin for up to four days or slice and freeze.

Soft rice bread

This is a moist loaf made with cooked long-grain rice added to the gluten-free flour mix. Its texture makes it particularly suitable for toasting, and it also keeps well in the fridge.

MAKES 1 LARGE LOAF

1 large egg

350 ml/12 fl oz /1$\frac{1}{3}$ cups water

15 g/$\frac{1}{2}$ oz/1 tbsp butter or margarine, melted

5 ml/1 tsp lemon juice

30 ml/2 tbsp dried milk powder (non-fat dry milk)

7.5 ml/1$\frac{1}{2}$ tsp salt

15 ml/1 tbsp caster (superfine) sugar

75 g/3 oz/$\frac{3}{4}$ cup cooked long-grain rice

350 g/12 oz/3 cups white gluten-free flour mix (see pages 11 and 12)

15 ml/1 tbsp xanthum gum

15 ml/1 tbsp active dried yeast

1 Beat together the egg and water, then pour into the breadmaker pan.

2 Add the melted butter or margarine, lemon juice, milk powder, salt, sugar and rice.

3 Add the flour and gum, then sprinkle the yeast on top.

4 Set the machine to Basic, 900 g/2 lb/Large, dark crust.

5 When cooked, switch off the machine and leave the bread to cool in the breadmaker for 10 minutes.

6 Turn the bread out of the pan on to a wire rack. When cool enough to handle, remove the paddle, if necessary.

7 When cold, store in the fridge for up to five days or slice and freeze.

Mixed seed bread

You need to be around when this loaf is cooking because it doesn't need the full pre-set cooking time. I always set a timer so I don't forget when I am busy with something else!

1 large egg

275 ml/9 fl oz/scant 1¼ cups milk

15 ml/1 tbsp sunflower oil

4 ml/¾ tsp salt

15 ml/1 tbsp caster (superfine) sugar

225 g/8 oz/2 cups white rice flour

10 ml/2 tsp xanthum gum

15 ml/1 tbsp pumpkin seeds

15 ml/1 tbsp sunflower seeds

15 ml/1 tbsp sesame seeds

1 sachet of easy-blend dried yeast

1 Beat together the egg and milk, then pour into the breadmaker pan.

2 Add all the remaining ingredients in the order listed.

3 Set the machine to Basic, 700 g/1½ lb/Medium, dark crust but cook for 40 minutes only or until golden and firm to the touch and shrinking slightly from the sides of the pan.

4 When cooked, switch off the machine and leave the bread to cool in the breadmaker for 10 minutes.

5 Turn the bread out of the pan onto a wire rack. When cool enough to handle, remove the paddle, if necessary.

6 When cold, store in the bread bin for up to four days or slice and freeze.

Farmhouse loaf

This rustic, floury-topped loaf is a delicious change from the other white breads. It's particularly good served with cheese and pickles for a Ploughman's lunch.

MAKES 1 MEDIUM LOAF

3 eggs

350 ml/12 fl oz/1⅓ cups water

60 ml/4 tbsp sunflower oil

5 ml/1 tsp distilled white vinegar

60 ml/4 tbsp dried milk powder (non-fat dry milk)

15 ml/1 tbsp clear honey

275 g/10 oz/2½ cups white rice flour

50 g/2 oz/½ cup potato flour

50 g/2 oz/½ cup buckwheat flour, plus extra for sprinkling

15 ml/1 tbsp xanthum gum

15 ml/1 tbsp caster (superfine) sugar

7.5 ml/1½ tsp salt

1 sachet of easy-blend dried yeast

1 Beat together the eggs and water, then pour into the breadmaker pan.

2 Add the oil, vinegar, milk powder and honey.

3 Add the flours, gum, sugar and salt, then sprinkle the yeast on top.

4 Set the machine to Basic, 700 g/1½ lb/Medium, medium crust.

5 When cooked, switch off the machine, sprinkle the bread immediately with a little buckwheat flour and leave in the breadmaker for 10 minutes.

6 Turn the bread out of the pan on to a wire rack. When cool enough to handle, remove the paddle, if necessary.

7 When cold, store in the bread bin for up to four days or slice and freeze.

Seeded farmhouse loaf

This loaf is made with a combination of brown rice flour, potato flour and buckwheat flour for a real farmhouse style. The addition of poppy seeds gives a surprisingly good nutty flavour.

MAKES 1 MEDIUM LOAF

3 eggs

350 ml/12 fl oz/1⅓ cups water

60 ml/4 tbsp sunflower oil

5 ml/1 tsp distilled white vinegar

60 ml/4 tbsp dried milk powder (non-fat dry milk)

15 ml/1 tbsp clear honey

275 g/10 oz/2½ cups brown rice flour

50 g/2 oz/½ cup potato flour

50 g/2 oz/½ cup buckwheat flour, plus extra for sprinkling

30 ml/2 tbsp poppy seeds

15 ml/1 tbsp xanthum gum

15 ml/1 tbsp caster (superfine) sugar

7.5 ml/1½ tsp salt

1 sachet of easy-blend dried yeast

1   Beat together the eggs and water, then pour into the breadmaker pan.

2   Add the oil, vinegar, milk powder and honey.

3   Add the flours, seeds, gum, sugar and salt, then sprinkle the yeast on top.

4   Set the machine to Basic, 700 g/1½ lb/Medium, medium crust.

5   When cooked, switch off the machine, sprinkle the bread immediately with a little buckwheat flour and leave in the breadmaker for 10 minutes.

6   Turn the bread out of the pan on to a wire rack. When cool enough to handle, remove the paddle, if necessary.

7   When cold, store in the bread bin for up to four days or slice and freeze.

White sandwich loaf

This large loaf with its soft crust is ideal for slicing for fresh or toasted sandwiches. You can use the Sandwich setting rather than Basic, if your machine has one, which will give a slightly thicker crust.

MAKES 1 LARGE LOAF

2 large eggs

550 ml/18 fl oz/2^1/$_3$ cups water

90 ml/6 tbsp dried milk powder (non-fat dry milk)

30 ml/2 tbsp sunflower oil

10 ml/2 tsp salt

30 ml/2 tbsp caster (superfine) sugar

450 g/1 lb/4 cups white rice flour

20 ml/1^1/$_2$ tbsp xanthum gum

20 ml/1^1/$_2$ tbsp active dried yeast

1 Beat together the eggs and water, then pour into the breadmaker pan.

2 Add all the remaining ingredients in the order listed.

3 Set the machine to Basic, 900 g/2 lb/Large.

4 When cooked, switch off the machine and leave the bread to cool in the breadmaker for 10 minutes.

5 Turn the bread out of the pan on to a wire rack. When cool enough to handle, remove the paddle, if necessary.

6 When cold, store in the bread bin for up to four days or slice and freeze.

Brown sandwich loaf

You can use 1 part buckwheat flour to 4 parts brown rice flour intead of the flour mix, if you prefer. Also, use the Sandwich setting if your machine has one.

MAKES 1 LARGE LOAF

2 large eggs

550 ml/18 fl oz /2¹/₃ cups water

75 ml/5 tbsp dried milk powder (non-fat dry milk)

10 ml/2 tsp distilled white vinegar

60 ml/4 tbsp sunflower oil

30 ml/2 tbsp light brown sugar

450 g/1 lb/4 cups brown gluten-free flour mix (see pages 11 and 12

20 ml/1¹/₂ tbsp xanthum gum

10 ml/2 tsp salt

20 ml/1¹/₂ tbsp active dried yeast

1 Beat together the egg, water and milk powder, then pour into the breadmaker pan.

2 Add the vinegar, oil and sugar.

3 Top with the flours, gum and salt.

4 Finally, sprinkle the yeast on top.

5 Set the machine to Basic, 900 g/2 lb/Large.

6 When cooked, switch off the machine and leave the bread to cool in the breadmaker for 10 minutes.

7 Turn the bread out of the pan on to a wire rack. When cool enough to handle, remove the paddle, if necessary.

8 When cold, store in the bread bin for up to four days or slice and freeze.

Multigrain loaf

This is an excellent high-fibre loaf with lots of flavour. Try ringing the changes with caraway and pumpkin seeds instead of linseed and sunflower seeds.

MAKES 1 MEDIUM LOAF

2 large eggs

350 ml/12 fl oz/1⅓ cups water

45 ml/3 tbsp dried milk powder (non-fat dry milk)

5 ml/1 tsp lemon juice

45 ml/3 tbsp sunflower oil

15 ml/1 tbsp golden (light corn) syrup

10 ml/2 tsp caster (superfine) sugar

350 g/12 oz/3 cups white gluten-free flour mix (see pages 11 and 12)

50 g/2 oz/½ cup gluten-free mixed grain cereal

10 ml/2 tsp linseed

10 ml/2 tsp poppy seeds

10 ml/2 tsp sunflower seeds

10 ml/2 tsp sesame seeds

15 ml/1 tbsp xanthum gum

7.5 ml/1½ tsp salt

15 ml/1 tbsp active dried yeast

1 Beat together the eggs, water and milk powder, then pour into the breadmaker pan.

2 Add the lemon juice, oil, syrup and sugar.

3 Top with the flour, cereal, seeds, gum and salt.

4 Finally, sprinkle the yeast on top.

5 Set the machine to Basic, 700 g/1½ lb/Medium, medium crust.

6 When cooked, switch off the machine and leave the bread to cool in the breadmaker for 10 minutes.

7 Turn the bread out of the pan on to a wire rack. When cool enough to handle, remove the paddle, if necessary.

8 When cold, store in the bread bin for up to four days or slice and freeze.

Flavoured Savoury Breads

All these breads make delectable sandwiches or a wonderful accompaniment to soups or salads. They are also a tasty lunch in themselves when sliced or cut into chunks and buttered.

Italian vegetable loaf

You can add the olives to this loaf in the fruit and nut dispenser if your breadmaker has one. Make sure you have dried them thoroughly first so they tip easily into the dough.

MAKES 1 MEDIUM LOAF

1 egg

350 ml/12 fl oz/1⅓ cups water

60 ml/4 tbsp olive oil

5 ml/1 tsp lemon juice

7.5 ml/1½ tsp garlic salt

20 ml/1½ tbsp caster (superfine) sugar

1 small courgette (zucchini), coarsely grated

1 small green (bell) pepper, coarsely grated

1 spring onion (scallion), finely chopped

400 g/14 oz/3½ cups white gluten-free flour mix (see pages 11 and 12)

10 ml/2 tsp Italian seasoning

15 ml/1 tbsp xanthum gum

15 ml/1 tbsp active dried yeast

50 g/2 oz/⅓ cup sliced black stoned (pitted) olives

1 Beat together the egg and water, then pour into the breadmaker pan.

2 Add the oil, lemon juice, garlic salt and sugar.

3 Squeeze the courgette and pepper thoroughly to remove the excess moisture. Add to the pan with the onion.

4 Add all the remaining ingredients except the olives, finishing with the yeast on top.

5 Set the machine to Basic, 700 g/1½ lb/Medium, dark crust.

6 Add the olives when the 10 beeps sound after the first knead.

7 When cooked, switch off the machine and leave the bread to cool in the breadmaker for 10 minutes. Turn out on to a wire rack. When cool enough to handle, remove the paddle, if necessary.

8 This loaf is best eaten fresh, or slice and freeze.

Pesto bread

This most Italian of breads tastes superb spread with unsalted butter, or topped with a slice or two of Mozzarella cheese and flashed under a hot grill until the cheese melts.

MAKES 1 MEDIUM LOAF

3 eggs

284 ml/9 fl oz/1 carton of buttermilk

75 ml/5 tbsp milk

10 ml/2 tsp lemon juice

20 ml/1½ tbsp clear honey

45 ml/3 tbsp ready-made pesto

15 ml/1 tbsp olive oil

5 ml/1 tsp salt

225 g/8 oz/2 cups white rice flour

25 g/1 oz/¼ cup cornflour (cornstarch)

50 g/2 oz/½ cup soya flour

50 g/2 oz/½ cup potato flour

15 ml/1 tbsp xanthum gum

15 ml/1 tbsp active dried yeast

1 Beat together the eggs, buttermilk and milk, then pour into the breadmaker pan.

2 Add the lemon juice, honey, pesto, oil and salt.

3 Mix together the flours and gum and add to the pan.

4 Finally, sprinkle the yeast on top.

5 Set the machine to Basic, 700 g/1½ lb/Medium, light or medium crust.

6 When cooked, switch off the machine and leave the bread to cool in the breadmaker for 10 minutes. Turn out on to a wire rack. When cool enough to handle, remove the paddle, if necessary.

7 When cold, store in the bread bin for up to four days or slice and freeze.

Cheddar cheese loaf

This loaf is delicious sliced and filled with salad or egg and mayonnaise for a light lunch. Try experimenting with other hard cheeses – like Red Leicester or even Stilton!

MAKES 1 MEDIUM LOAF

1 egg

350 ml/12 fl oz/1⅓ cups water

60 ml/4 tbsp sunflower oil

5 ml/1 tsp lemon juice

7.5 ml/1½ tsp salt

20 ml/1½ tbsp caster (superfine) sugar

75 g/3 oz/¾ cup grated strong Cheddar cheese

2.5 ml/½ tsp gluten-free English mustard powder (optional)

350 g/12 oz/3 cups white gluten-free flour mix (see pages 11 and 12)

15 ml/1 tbsp xanthum gum

15 ml/1 tbsp active dried yeast

1 Beat together the egg and water, then pour into the breadmaker pan.

2 Add all the remaining ingredients in the order listed.

3 Set the machine to Basic, 700 g/1½ lb/Medium, medium crust.

4 When cooked, switch off the machine and leave the bread to cool in the breadmaker for 10 minutes. Turn out on to a wire rack. When cool enough to handle, remove the paddle, if necessary.

5 This loaf is best eaten warm. Store in the bread bin for up to four days or slice and freeze.

Savoury pecan bread

*You can add the nuts to this loaf in the fruit and
nut dispenser if your breadmaker has one.
Substitute walnuts and ordinary golden syrup
if you prefer.*

MAKES 1 MEDIUM LOAF

1 large egg

350 ml/12 fl oz/1⅓ cups water

45 ml/3 tbsp dried milk powder
(non-fat dry milk)

5 ml/1 tsp lemon juice

45 ml/3 tbsp sunflower oil

20 ml/1½ tbsp maple syrup

350 g/12 oz/3 cups brown rice
flour

15 ml/1 tbsp xanthum gum

7.5 ml/1½ tsp salt

15 ml/1 tbsp active dried yeast

50 g/2 oz/½ cup pecans,
chopped

1 Beat together the egg, water and milk powder, then pour
into the breadmaker pan.

2 Add the lemon juice, oil and maple syrup.

3 Top with the flour, gum and salt.

4 Finally, sprinkle the yeast on top.

5 Set the machine to Basic, 700 g/1½ lb/Medium, dark
crust.

6 Add the nuts when the 10 beeps sound after the first
knead.

7 When cooked, switch off the machine and leave the
bread to cool in the breadmaker for 10 minutes. Turn
out on to a wire rack. When cool enough to handle,
remove the paddle, if necessary.

8 When cool, store in the bread bin for up to four days or
slice and freeze.

Danish blue bread

The nuts and celery can be added in the fruit and nut dispenser if your breadmaker has one.
Try using strong grated Cheddar cheese for a change from Danish Blue too.

MAKES 1 MEDIUM LOAF

1 large egg

400 ml/14 fl oz/1¾ cups water

15 ml/1 tbsp dried milk powder (non-fat dry milk)

5 ml/1 tsp lemon juice

30 ml/2 tbsp sunflower oil

15 ml/1 tbsp black treacle (molasses)

100 g/4 oz/1 cup crumbled Danish Blue cheese

350 g/12 oz/3 cups brown rice flour

15 ml/1 tbsp xanthum gum

7.5 ml/1½ tsp salt

15 ml/1 tbsp active dried yeast

75 g/3 oz/¾ cup chopped walnuts

2 celery sticks, finely chopped

1 Beat together the egg, water and milk powder, then pour into the breadmaker pan.

2 Add the lemon juice, oil, treacle and cheese.

3 Top with the flour, gum and salt.

4 Finally, sprinkle the yeast on top.

5 Set the machine to Basic, 700 g/1½ lb/Medium, medium crust.

6 Add the nuts and celery when the 10 beeps sound after the first knead.

7 When cooked, switch off the machine and leave the bread to cool in the breadmaker for 10 minutes. Turn out on to a wire rack. When cool enough to handle, remove the paddle, if necessary.

8 Serve warm or cold. Store in the bread bin for up to four days or slice and freeze.

Tapenade loaf

*This is another lovely Mediterranean-style loaf.
It's delicious with vegetable soups, like minestrone,
as an accompaniment to pasta dishes or just to
enjoy with butter.*

MAKES 1 MEDIUM LOAF

3 eggs

284 ml/9 fl oz/1 carton of buttermilk

75 ml/5 tbsp milk

5 ml/1 tsp lemon juice

20 ml/1½ tbsp golden (light corn) syrup

45 ml/3 tbsp ready-made tapenade

15 ml/1 tbsp olive oil

5 ml/1 tsp salt

225 g/8 oz/2 cups brown rice flour

25 g/1 oz/¼ cup cornflour (cornstarch)

50 g/2 oz/½ cup soya flour

50 g/2 oz/½ cup potato flour

15 ml/1 tbsp xanthum gum

15 ml/1 tbsp active dried yeast

1 Beat together the eggs, buttermilk and milk, then pour into the breadmaker pan.

2 Add the lemon juice, syrup, tapenade, oil and salt.

3 Mix together the flours and gum and add to the pan.

4 Finally, sprinkle the yeast on top.

5 Set the machine to Basic, 700 g/1½ lb/Medium, light or medium crust.

6 When cooked, switch off the machine and leave the bread to cool in the breadmaker for 10 minutes. Turn out on to a wire rack. When cool enough to handle, remove the paddle, if necessary.

7 When cold, store in the bread bin for up to four days or slice and freeze.

Salt and pepper bread

This simple savoury loaf is a delicious accompaniment to any main meal. It's equally good sliced and buttered or, Mediterranean-style, drizzled with olive oil.

MAKES 1 MEDIUM LOAF

1 large egg

350 ml/12 fl oz/1⅓ cups milk

20 ml/1½ tbsp sunflower oil

5 ml/1 tsp salt

20 ml/1½ tbsp caster (superfine) sugar

350 g/12 oz/3 cups brown rice flour

15 ml/1 tbsp xanthum gum

30 ml/2 tbsp coarsely crushed black peppercorns

1 sachet of easy-blend dried yeast

15 ml/1 tbsp coarse sea salt

1 Beat together the egg and milk, then pour into the breadmaker pan.

2 Add all the remaining ingredients except the sea salt in the order listed.

3 Set the machine to Basic, 700 g/1½ lb/Medium, medium crust.

4 When the loaf starts to cook – 1 hour before the end of the programme – gently open the lid as little as possible and sprinkle the sea salt over the surface, then gently close the lid again.

5 When cooked, switch off the machine, leave the loaf in the breadmaker for 10 minutes, then turn it out on to a wire rack. When cool enough to handle, remove the paddle, if necessary.

6 When cool, store in the bread bin for up to four days or slice and freeze.

Sun-dried tomato bread

You can add two or three chopped sun-dried tomatoes to the mixture for added flavour and texture if you like. For a more everyday loaf, use ordinary tomato purée and lift the flavour by adding 5 ml/1 tsp dried basil.

MAKES 1 MEDIUM LOAF

3 eggs

284 ml/9 fl oz/1 carton of buttermilk

75 ml/5 tbsp milk

10 ml/2 tsp lemon juice

20 ml/1½ tbsp clear honey

45 ml/3 tbsp sun-dried tomato purée (paste)

15 ml/1 tbsp olive oil

5 ml/1 tsp salt

375 g/13 oz/3¼ cups white gluten-free flour mix (see pages 11 and 12)

15 ml/1 tbsp xanthum gum

15 ml/1 tbsp active dried yeast

1 Beat together the eggs, buttermilk and milk, then pour into the breadmaker pan.

2 Add the lemon juice, honey, sun-dried tomato purée, oil and salt.

3 Mix together the flour and gum and add to the pan.

4 Finally, sprinkle the yeast on top.

5 Set the machine to Basic, 700 g/1½ lb/Medium, light or medium crust.

6 When cooked, switch off the machine and leave the bread to cool in the breadmaker for 10 minutes. Turn out on to a wire rack. When cool enough to handle, remove the paddle, if necessary.

7 When cold, store in the bread bin for up to four days or slice and freeze.

Mustard seed loaf

This tasty loaf has a nutty flavour and a lovely soft, doughy texture that is great simply spread with butter.
It also makes fabulous sandwiches, especially filled with ham or beef.

MAKES 1 MEDIUM LOAF

15 ml/1 tbsp sunflower oil

30 ml/2 tbsp black mustard seeds

1 large egg

275 ml/9 fl oz/scant 1¼ cups milk

4 ml/¾ tsp salt

15 ml/1 tbsp caster (superfine) sugar

225 g/8 oz/2 cups white rice flour

10 ml/2 tsp xanthum gum

1 sachet of easy-blend dried yeast

1   Heat the oil in a small saucepan. Add the mustard seeds and heat until they start to 'pop', then remove the pan from the heat.

2   Beat together the egg and milk, then pour into the breadmaker pan and add the seeds in their oil.

3   Add all the remaining ingredients in the order listed.

4   Set the machine to Basic, 700 g/1½ lb/Medium, dark crust but allow to cook for 40 minutes only or until golden and firm to the touch and shrinking slightly from the sides of the pan.

5   When cooked, switch off the machine and leave the bread to cool in the breadmaker for 10 minutes.

6   Turn the bread out of the pan on to a wire rack. When cool enough to handle, remove the paddle, if necessary.

7   When cold, store in the bread bin for up to four days or slice and freeze.

Sage pancetta bread

You can use 225 g/8 oz of leftover boiled potato for this recipe instead of cooking a potato. Pancetta is available in most supermarkets, but you could use ordinary bacon instead.

MAKES 1 LARGE LOAF

1 large unpeeled potato, scrubbed and pricked with a fork

100 g/4 oz/1 cup diced pancetta

2 large eggs

275 ml/9 fl oz/scant 1¼ cups water

50 g/2 oz/¼ cup butter or margarine, melted

5 ml/1 tsp distilled white vinegar

30 ml/2 tbsp caster (superfine) sugar

15 ml/1 tbsp chopped fresh sage, or 5 ml/1 tsp dried

225 g/8 oz/2 cups white rice flour

50 g/2 oz/½ cup tapioca flour

100 g/4 oz/1 cup potato flour

4 ml/¾ tsp salt

10 ml/2 tsp powdered gelatine

15 ml/1 tbsp xanthum gum

20 ml/1½ tbsp active dried yeast

1 Boil the potato whole for about 20 minutes or bake in the microwave for about 4 minutes until soft. Drain and cool, then peel off the skin. Mash thoroughly.

2 Dry-fry the pancetta in a frying pan (skillet), stirring until golden and fairly crisp. Set aside.

3 Beat together the eggs and water, then pour into the breadmaker pan.

4 Add the mashed potato, then all the remaining ingredients in the order listed, finishing with the yeast on top.

5 Set the machine to Basic, 900 g/2 lb/Large, medium crust.

6 Add the pancetta and any oil in the pan when the 10 beeps sound after the first knead.

7 When cooked, switch off the machine and leave the bread to cool in the breadmaker for 10 minutes. Turn out on to a wire rack. When cool enough to handle, remove the paddle, if necessary.

8 The bread is best eaten fresh or slice and freeze.

Pisaladière

This cinnamon-flavoured crust, spread with a rich tomato filling and topped with anchovies, makes a delicious starter, lunch or supper dish. Serve it warm for the best flavour. You can make two smaller pies if you wish.

SERVES 4–8

120 ml/4 fl oz/½ cup milk

100 ml/3½ fl oz/scant ½ cup plain yoghurt

1 egg

60 ml/4 tbsp olive oil, plus extra for greasing

350 g/12 oz/3 cups white gluten-free flour mix (see pages 11 and 12)

15 ml/1 tbsp caster (superfine) sugar

4 ml/¾ tsp salt

2.5 ml/½ tsp gluten-free baking powder

5 ml/1 tsp ground cinnamon

10 ml/2 tsp easy-blend dried yeast

3 onions, chopped

1 garlic clove, crushed

400 g/14 oz/1 large can of chopped tomatoes

15 ml/1 tbsp tomato purée (paste)

Salt and freshly ground black pepper

50 g/2 oz/1 small can of anchovies, drained

A few black olives

15 ml/1 tbsp chopped fresh parsley

1 Warm the milk and yoghurt together in a saucepan until comfortably warm to the touch but not hot. Remove from the heat and whisk in the eggs then pour into the breadmaker pan. Add half the oil.

2 Sift the flour with 10 ml/2 tsp of the sugar, the salt, baking powder and cinnamon. Tip into the pan and sprinkle the yeast on top.

3 Set the machine to Dough. When the dough has kneaded but has not yet started to heat and rise, switch off the machine.

4 Press the dough into a large (33 cm/13½ in diameter) oiled pizza pan. Leave in a warm place for 30 minutes to prove.

5 Meanwhile, preheat the oven to 200°C/400°F/gas 6/fan oven 180°C.

6 Bake the base for 10 minutes.

7 Meanwhile, heat the remaining oil in a saucepan. Add the onions and garlic and fry (sauté), stirring, for 3 minutes to soften. Add the tomatoes, tomato purée and the remaining sugar and season to taste with salt and pepper. Bring to the boil and boil rapidly for 5 minutes, stirring occasionally, until pulpy.

8 Spoon the tomato mixture over the bread case. Arrange the anchovies in a lattice pattern on top. Dot with the olives in the spaces.

9 Return to the oven for about 20 minutes until the dough is golden round the edges. Sprinkle with the parsley.

10 Serve warm.

Mexican chilli bread

As you might expect, with its spicy Mexican flavour this loaf is fabulous served with an avocado dip. You can also slice it for sandwiches and fill them with your favourite salad ingredients.

MAKES 1 LARGE LOAF

2 eggs

400 ml/14 fl oz/1¾ cups water

30 ml/2 tbsp tomato purée (paste)

60 ml/4 tbsp sunflower oil

5 ml/1 tsp distilled white vinegar

20 ml/1½ tbsp caster (superfine) sugar

10 ml/2 tsp salt

60 ml/4 tbsp dried milk powder (non-fat dry milk)

150 g/5 oz/1¼ cups brown rice flour

150 g/5 oz/1¼ cups white rice flour

100 g/4 oz/1 cup potato flour

50 g/2 oz/½ cup soya flour

15 ml/1 tbsp xanthum gum

10 ml/2 tsp chilli powder

1 green chilli, seeded and finely chopped

30 ml/2 tbsp chopped fresh coriander (cilantro)

20 ml/1½ tbsp active dried yeast

1 Beat together the eggs, water and tomato purée, then pour into the breadmaker pan.

2 Add the oil, vinegar, sugar, salt and milk powder.

3 Mix together the flours, gum and chilli powder and add to the breadmaker with the chopped chilli and coriander.

4 Finally, sprinkle the yeast on top.

5 Set the machine to Basic, 900 g/2 lb/Large, medium crust.

6 When cooked, switch off the machine and leave the bread to cool in the breadmaker for 10 minutes. Turn out on to a wire rack. When cool enough to handle, remove the paddle, if necessary.

7 Serve warm or cold. Store in the bread bin for up to four days or slice and freeze.

Speciality Breads

~

These are all a little bit different for when you're feeling adventurous. Some of them require you to make the dough in the breadmaker then, when proved and kneaded, you remove it, shape it and bake it in a conventional oven. The breadmaker does all the hard work, leaving you to create the masterpieces!

Some of these doughs need spraying with water during preparation. I use the same water spray I keep for dampening over-dry washing and you can do the same, but make sure you always use fresh water!

Focaccia bread

This bread is always best served fresh but you can freeze it.
If you do, it can be reheated briefly in the microwave
or warmed in the oven from frozen when you
are ready to serve.

MAKES 1 ROUND LOAF

1 egg

350 ml/12 fl oz/1⅓ cups warm but not hot water

75 ml/5 tbsp olive oil

5 ml/1 tsp lemon juice

400 g/14 oz/3½ cups white gluten-free flour mix (see pages 11 and 12), plus extra for dusting

7.5 ml/1½ tsp salt

20 ml/1½ tbsp caster (superfine) sugar

15 ml/1 tbsp xanthum gum

1 sachet of easy-blend dried yeast

5 ml/1 tsp coarse sea salt

1 Beat together the egg and warm water, then pour into the breadmaker pan with 60 ml/4 tbsp of the oil. Add the lemon juice.

2 Mix together the flour, salt, sugar and gum, then tip into the pan. Finally, sprinkle the yeast on top.

3 Set the machine to Dough. Brush a 20 cm/8 in loose-bottomed cake tin (pan) with a little olive oil.

4 When the dough has kneaded but has not yet started to heat and rise (about 20 minutes, depending on the model), tip it out of the breadmaker on to a board dusted with a little more flour. Re-knead lightly, then press gently into the prepared tin.

5 Spray the dough lightly with water. Cover the tin with oiled clingfilm (plastic wrap) and leave to prove in a warm place for about 45 minutes until doubled in size.

6 Meanwhile, preheat the oven to 220°C/425°F/gas 7/fan oven 190°C.

7   Using a finger dusted in flour, make several dimples in the surface of the risen dough. Drizzle with the remaining olive oil and sprinkle with coarse sea salt. Spray lightly with water again.

8   Bake in the oven for about 45 minutes until pale golden and cooked through. Spray twice with water during cooking to keep the crust soft.

9   Transfer to a wire rack and cover with a damp tea towel to keep the crust soft. Serve while still warm.

Rosemary focaccia

*This loaf smells so fantastic while it's cooking, it's hard to
let it cool enough to cut when you turn it out!
Resist the temptation for 10 minutes, though, or
you'll get a doughy result.*

MAKES 1 ROUND LOAF

1 egg

350 ml/12 fl oz/1⅓ cups warm
but not hot water

75 ml/5 tbsp olive oil, plus extra
for brushing

5 ml/1 tsp lemon juice

400 g/14 oz/3½ cups white
gluten-free flour mix (see pages
11 and 12), plus extra for
dusting

7.5 ml/1½ tsp garlic salt

20 ml/1½ tbsp caster (superfine)
sugar

15 ml/1 tbsp xanthum gum

10 ml/2 tsp finely chopped fresh
rosemary

1 sachet of easy-blend dried yeast

1 onion, thinly sliced

5 ml/1 tsp coarse sea salt

1 Beat together the egg and warm water, then pour into the
breadmaker pan with 60 ml/4 tbsp of the oil. Add the
lemon juice.

2 Mix together the flour, salt, sugar and gum, then tip into
the pan. Add the rosemary. Finally, sprinkle the yeast on
top.

3 Set the machine to Dough. Brush a 20 cm/8 in loose-
bottomed cake tin (pan) with a little olive oil.

4 When the dough has kneaded but has not yet started to
heat and rise (about 20 minutes, depending on the
model), tip it out of the breadmaker on to a board
dusted with a little more flour. Re-knead lightly, then
press gently into the prepared tin.

5 Spray the dough lightly with water. Cover the tin with
oiled clingfilm (plastic wrap) and leave to prove in a
warm place for about 45 minutes until the dough has
doubled in size.

6 Meanwhile, preheat the oven to 220°C/425°F/gas 7/fan oven 190°C.

7 Using a finger dusted in flour, make several dimples in the surface of the risen dough. Mix the onion with the remaining olive oil and scatter over the surface. Sprinkle with coarse sea salt. Spray lightly with water again.

8 Bake in the oven for about 45 minutes until pale golden and cooked through. Spray twice with water during cooking to keep the crust soft.

9 Transfer to a wire rack and cover with a damp tea towel to keep the crust soft. Serve while still warm.

Tomato focaccia

*This full-of-flavour bread gives you a real taste of Italy.
Enjoy it with any pasta, risotto or soup or as an
accompaniment to grilled or roasted meat,
poultry or fish.*

MAKES 1 ROUND LOAF

10 fresh basil leaves

1 egg

350 ml/12 fl oz/1⅓ cups warm but not hot water

60 ml/4 tbsp olive oil

15 ml/1 tbsp sun-dried tomato oil from the jar

5 ml/1 tsp lemon juice

400 g/14 oz/3½ cups white gluten-free flour mix (see pages 11 and 12)

7.5 ml/1½ tsp salt

20 ml/1½ tbsp caster (superfine) sugar

15 ml/1 tbsp xanthum gum

1 sachet of easy-blend dried yeast

3 pieces of sun-dried tomato in oil, drained and roughly chopped

A little cornflour (cornstarch) for dusting

50 g/2 oz/⅓ cup sliced black or green stoned (pitted) olives

1 Finely chop half the basil and put in the breadmaker pan. Beat together the egg and warm water, then pour into the pan with 45 ml/3 tbsp of the olive oil and the tomato oil. Add the lemon juice.

2 Mix together the flour, salt, sugar and gum, then tip into the pan.

3 Finally, sprinkle the yeast on top.

4 Set the machine to Dough. Brush a 20 cm/8 in loose-bottomed cake tin (pan) with a little olive oil.

5 When the dough has kneaded but has not yet started to heat and rise (about 20 minutes, depending on the model), tip it out of the breadmaker onto a board dusted with a little more flour. Re-knead lightly then press gently into the prepared tin.

6 Scatter the sun-dried tomatoes over the dough. Spray lightly with water, cover the tin with oiled clingfilm (plastic wrap) and leave to prove in a warm place for about 45 minutes until the dough has doubled in size.

7 Meanwhile, preheat the oven to 220°C/425°F/gas 7/fan oven 190°C.

8 Using a finger dusted in cornflour, make several dimples in the surface of the risen dough. Tear the remaining basil leaves into pieces and sprinkle over with the olive slices. Drizzle with the remaining olive oil and spray lightly with water again.

9 Bake in the oven for about 45 minutes until pale golden and cooked through. Spray twice with water during cooking to keep the crust soft.

10 Transfer to a wire rack and cover with a damp tea towel to keep the crust soft. Serve while still warm.

Pizza marguerita

How many this amount of dough will serve depends on individual appetites – my family can eat a whole one of these each! Your breadmaker will make double the quantity of dough for four large ones if you require more.

MAKES 2

For the dough:

250 ml/8 fl oz/1 cup water

30 ml/2 tbsp olive oil, plus extra for greasing

175 g/6 oz/1½ cups white or brown rice flour

50 g/2 oz/½ cup tapioca flour

100 g/4 oz/1 cup potato flour

15 g/½ oz/2 tbsp cornflour (cornstarch), plus extra for dusting

10 ml/2 tsp xanthum gum

4 ml/¾ tsp salt

10 ml/2 tsp caster (superfine) sugar

10 ml/2 tsp easy-blend dried yeast

For the topping:

90 ml/6 tbsp tomato purée (paste)

5 ml/1 tsp dried basil or oregano

200 g/7 oz/1¾ cups grated Mozzarella cheese

4 tomatoes, sliced

30 ml/2 tbsp olive oil

A few torn fresh basil leaves

Freshly ground black pepper

A few black olives for garnishing (optional)

1   To make the dough, put the water and oil in the breadmaker pan.

2   Add the flours, gum, salt and sugar, then sprinkle the yeast on top.

3   Set the machine to Dough.

4   When the dough has kneaded and proved, tip it out on to a surface dusted with cornflour. Re-knead briefly. Divide the dough in half and place on two oiled baking (cookie) sheets. Press each piece out to a thin round about 28 cm/11 in diameter.

5   Preheat the oven to 220°C/425°F/gas 7/fan oven 200°C.

6 Spread the dough gently with the tomato purée, then sprinkle with the basil or oregano. Top with the cheese, then the tomato slices. Drizzle the olive oil over and scatter with a few torn basil leaves. Add a good grinding of pepper and garnish with olives, if liked.

7 Bake for about 20 minutes until crisp and golden round the edges and the cheese is bubbling and turning golden in places.

Pizza la reine

This is another very popular topping for a pizza. You can use ordinary streaky bacon instead of the pancetta if you like or, alternatively, use diced cooked ham but there is no need to fry it first – just lightly cook the mushrooms.

MAKES 2

For the dough:

250 ml/8 fl oz/1 cup water

30 ml/2 tbsp olive oil, plus extra for greasing

175 g/6 oz/1½ cups white or brown rice flour

50 g/2 oz/½ cup tapioca flour

100 g/4 oz/1 cup potato flour

15 g/½ oz/2 tbsp cornflour (cornstarch), plus extra for dusting

10 ml/2 tsp xanthum gum

4 ml/¾ tsp salt

10 ml/2 tsp sugar

10 ml/2 tsp easy-blend dried yeast

For the topping:

100 g/4 oz/1 cup diced pancetta

100 g/4 oz button mushrooms, sliced

30 ml/2 tbsp olive oil

90 ml/6 tbsp tomato purée (paste)

5 ml/1 tsp dried oregano

200 g/7 oz/1¾ cups grated Mozzarella cheese

Freshly ground black pepper

A few black olives for garnishing (optional)

1 To make the dough, put the water and oil in the breadmaker pan.

2 Add the flours, gum, salt and sugar, then sprinkle the yeast on top.

3 Set the machine to Dough.

4 When the dough has kneaded and proved, tip it out on to a surface dusted with cornflour. Re-knead briefly. Divide the dough in half and place on two oiled baking (cookie) sheets. Press each piece out to a thin round about 28 cm/11 in diameter.

5 Preheat the oven to 220°C/425°F/gas 7/fan oven 200°C.

6 To make the topping, fry (sauté) the pancetta and mushrooms in half the olive oil for 2 minutes, stirring, until lightly cooked.

7 Spread the dough gently with the tomato purée, then sprinkle with the oregano. Top with the pancetta and mushrooms (including any juices), then the cheese. Drizzle the remaining olive oil over, add a good grinding of pepper and garnish with olives, if liked.

8 Bake for about 20 minutes until crisp and golden round the edges and the cheese is bubbling and turning golden in places.

Jalapeño beef pizza

This is a hot and spicy Mexican-style pizza, perfect for anyone who loves those chilli flavours – it makes a fabulous TV dinner! You can easily alter the quantities to make more if you like.

MAKES 2

For the dough:

250 ml/8 fl oz/1 cup water

30 ml/2 tbsp olive oil, plus extra for greasing

175 g/6 oz/1½ cups white or brown rice flour

50 g/2 oz/½ cup tapioca flour

100 g/4 oz/1 cup potato flour

15 g/½ oz/2 tbsp cornflour (cornstarch), plus extra for dusting

10 ml/2 tsp xanthum gum

4 ml/¾ tsp salt

10 ml/2 tsp sugar

10 ml/2 tsp easy-blend dried yeast

For the topping:

100 g/4 oz minced (ground) beef

30 ml/2 tbsp minced dried onion

1 garlic clove, crushed

2.5 ml/½ tsp ground cumin

2.5 ml/½ tsp chilli powder

120 ml/4 fl oz/½ cup tomato purée (paste)

2.5 ml/½ tsp caster (superfine) sugar

Salt and freshly ground black pepper

5 ml/1 tsp dried oregano

2 pickled jalapeño peppers, sliced

175 g/6 oz/1½ cups grated Mozzarella cheese

30 ml/2 tbsp olive oil

A few black olives for garnishing (optional)

1 To make the dough, put the water and oil in the breadmaker pan.

2 Add the flours, gum, salt and sugar, then sprinkle the yeast on top.

3 Set the machine to Dough.

4 When the dough has kneaded and proved, tip it out on to a surface dusted with cornflour. Re-knead briefly. Divide the dough in half and place on two oiled baking

(cookie) sheets. Press each piece out to a thin round about 28 cm/11 in diameter.

5 Preheat the oven to 220°C/425°F/gas 7/fan oven 200°C.

6 To make the topping, dry-fry the mince in a saucepan with the minced onion and garlic, stirring until the beef grains are separate and no longer pink. Stir in the spices and cook, stirring, for 1 minute. Add 30 ml/2 tbsp of the tomato purée, the sugar and salt and pepper to taste.

7 Spread the dough gently with the remaining tomato purée, then sprinkle with the oregano. Spread the meat mixture over the top and scatter with the pepper slices. Scatter the cheese on top and drizzle with the olive oil. Garnish with olives, if liked.

8 Bake for about 20 minutes until crisp and golden round the edges and the cheese is bubbling and turning golden in places.

French bread

If you don't have a baguette baking tin, shape a container out of double-thickness heavy-duty foil to about 30 cm/12 in × 10 cm/4 in and about 7.5 cm/3 in deep and stand it on a baking (cookie) sheet.

MAKES 1 LOAF

2 egg whites

375 ml/13 fl oz /1½ cups water

5 ml/1 tsp lemon juice

350 g/12 oz/3 cups white gluten-free flour mix (see pages 11 and 12)

15 ml/1 tbsp xanthum gum

10 ml/2 tsp caster (superfine) sugar

7.5 ml/1½ tsp salt

1 sachet of easy-blend dried yeast

A little milk for glazing

10 ml/2 tsp poppy seeds (optional)

1 Whisk the egg whites until fairly frothy, then whisk in the water and lemon juice. Tip into the breadmaker pan.

2 Mix together the flour, gum, sugar and salt, then tip into the pan. Sprinkle the yeast on top.

3 Set the machine to Dough. When the dough has kneaded but has not yet started to heat and rise (about 20 minutes, depending on the model), turn it out into an oiled French baguette baking tin and spread evenly.

4 Cover loosely with oiled clingfilm (plastic wrap) and leave to prove in a warm place for about 1 hour until the mixture has doubled in size.

5 Meanwhile, preheat the oven to 200°C/400°F/gas 6/fan oven 180°C.

6 Using a sharp knife, gently make several little diagonal slashes across the loaf at intervals. Brush with a little milk to glaze and sprinkle with poppy seeds, if liked.

7 Bake the loaf for about 40 minutes until crisp and golden. Leave to cool in the tin for 15 minutes, then remove. Best served warm.

Garlic French bread

You can also make an ordinary-shaped loaf on the French Bread setting, if your machine has one, or shape a container as in the French Bread recipe opposite.

MAKES 1 LOAF

2 egg whites

375 ml/13 fl oz /1½ cups water

5 ml/1 tsp lemon juice

1 large garlic clove, crushed

45 ml/3 tbsp chopped fresh parsley

350 g/12 oz/3 cups white gluten-free flour mix (see pages 11 and 12)

15 ml/1 tbsp xanthum gum

10 ml/2 tsp caster (superfine) sugar

7.5 ml/1½ tsp salt

1 sachet of easy-blend dried yeast

A little milk for glazing

5 ml/1 tsp sesame seeds (optional)

1 Whisk the egg whites until fairly frothy, then whisk in the water, lemon juice, garlic and parsley. Tip into the breadmaker pan.

2 Mix together the flour, gum, sugar and salt, then tip into the pan. Sprinkle the yeast on top.

3 Set the machine to Dough. When the dough has kneaded but has not yet started to heat and rise (about 20 minutes, depending on the model), turn it out into an oiled French baguette baking tin and spread evenly.

4 Cover loosely with oiled clingfilm (plastic wrap) and leave to prove in a warm place for about 1 hour until the mixture has doubled in size.

5 Meanwhile, preheat the oven to 200°C/400°F/gas 6/fan oven 180°C.

6 Using a sharp knife, gently make several little diagonal slashes across the loaf at intervals. Brush with a little milk to glaze and sprinkle with sesame seeds, if liked.

7 Bake the loaf for about 40 minutes until crisp and golden. Leave to cool in the tin or foil for 15 minutes, then remove. Best served warm.

Pumpernickel

*This does not contain rye flour, which is the basis
for traditional pumpernickel, but it tastes
pretty authentic nonetheless!
Enjoy it with fresh unsalted butter.*

MAKES 1 MEDIUM LOAF

40 g/1½ oz/3 tbsp quinoa grains

5 ml/1 tsp instant coffee granules

300 ml/½ pt/1¼ cups water

1 large egg

5 ml/1 tsp malt vinegar

30 ml/2 tbsp sunflower oil

10 ml/2 tsp clear honey

15 ml/1 tbsp black treacle
(molasses)

5 ml/1 tsp salt

50 g/2 oz/½ cup tapioca flour

40 g/1½ oz/⅓ cup soya flour

150 g/5 oz/1¼ cups brown rice
flour

25 g/1 oz/¼ cup maize flour

30 ml/2 tbsp gluten-free cocoa
(unsweetened chocolate)
powder

10 ml/2 tsp xanthum gum

10 ml/2 tsp caraway seeds

10 ml/2 tsp active dried yeast

1 Boil the quinoa in plenty of water for 15 minutes, then
   drain thoroughly.

2 Dissolve the coffee in the measured water, then whisk in
   the egg. Tip into the breadmaker pan. Add the vinegar,
   oil, honey, treacle and salt.

3 Mix together the flours, cocoa powder and gum and add
   to the pan with the quinoa. Sprinkle the caraway seeds
   on top, then the yeast.

4 Set the machine to Basic, 700 g/1½ lb/Medium, medium
   crust.

5 When cooked, leave in the breadmaker for 10 minutes
   then turn the loaf out on to a wire rack. When cool
   enough to handle, remove the paddle, if necessary.

6 This loaf keeps well in the fridge for several days or can
   be sliced and frozen.

Brioche

This gluten-free brioche is perhaps not quite as light as 'the real thing' but it's an exceptionally good loaf just the same. Enjoy it for a continental breakfast with unsalted butter and pure fruit conserve or honey.

MAKES 1 MEDIUM LOAF

4 eggs

175 ml/6 fl oz/³/₄ cup water

45 ml/3 tbsp rum

50 g/2 oz/¹/₄ cup butter, melted

60 ml/4 tbsp caster (superfine) sugar

2.5 ml/¹/₂ tsp salt

175 g/6 oz/1¹/₂ cups soya flour

175 g/6 oz/1¹/₂ cups white gluten-free flour mix (see pages 11 and 12)

50 g/2 oz/¹/₂ cup cornflour (cornstarch)

5 ml/1 tsp baking powder

15 ml/1 tbsp active dried yeast

A little beaten egg or an egg yolk beaten with 10 ml/2 tsp water for glazing

1 Beat together the eggs, water and rum, then pour into the breadmaker.

2 Add the melted butter, sugar and salt.

3 Sift together the flours and baking powder, then tip into the pan.

4 Finally, sprinkle the yeast on top.

5 Set the machine to Basic, 700 g/1¹/₂ lb/Medium, light crust.

6 When the dough has kneaded and risen, before cooking, quickly lift the lid and brush the surface very gently with the egg glaze. Close the lid carefully.

7 When cooked, leave in the breadmaker for 15 minutes, then turn out on to a wire rack. Remove the paddle, if necessary, and leave to cool.

8 This brioche is best eaten within two days, or slice and freeze.

Panettone

This lovely, light loaf is traditionally eaten at Christmas but it is delicious sliced and spread with butter for breakfast or even for a tea time treat any time of the year. Use the fruit and nut dispenser if your machine has one.

MAKES 1 MEDIUM LOAF

3 eggs

350 ml/12 fl oz/1⅓ cups water

60 ml/4 tbsp dried milk powder (non-fat dry milk)

15 ml/1 tbsp clear honey

50 g/2 oz/¼ cup butter or margarine, melted

Finely grated zest and juice of 1 small orange

100 g/4 oz/1 cup tapioca flour

100 g/4 oz/1 cup white rice flour

100 g/4 oz/1 cup potato flour

15 ml/1 tbsp cornflour (cornstarch)

100 g/4 oz/1 cup ground almonds

10 ml/2 tsp xanthum gum

7.5 ml/1½ tsp powdered gelatine

2.5 ml/½ tsp bicarbonate of soda (baking soda)

50 g/2 oz/¼ cup caster (superfine) sugar

1 sachet of easy-blend dried yeast

40 g/1½ oz/⅓ cup chopped mixed nuts or pine nuts

25 g/1 oz/3 tbsp chopped mixed (candied) peel

40 g/1½ oz/¼ cup sultanas (golden raisins)

A little icing (confectioners') sugar for dusting

1 Beat together the eggs and water, then pour into the breadmaker pan.

2 Add the milk powder, honey, melted butter or margarine and the orange zest and juice.

3 Add the flours, then the ground almonds, gum, gelatine, bicarbonate of soda and sugar. Tip into the pan.

4 Finally, sprinkle the yeast on top.

5 Set the machine to Basic, 700 g/1½ lb/Medium, light crust.

6 Add the chopped nuts, peel and sultanas when the 10 beeps sound after the first knead.

7 When cooked, switch off the machine and leave in the breadmaker for 10 minutes, then turn out on to a wire rack. When cool enough to handle, remove the paddle, if necessary. Dust with a little sifted icing sugar.

8 This loaf is best eaten within three days, or slice and freeze.

Stollen

Another popular continental loaf served at Christmas time.
We enjoy it at Easter too and, of course, you could
have it any time. It's particularly good with
rich espresso coffee.

1 egg

300 ml/¹/₂ pt /1¹/₄ cups warm but not hot milk

50 g/2 oz/¹/₄ cup butter, melted

40 g/1¹/₂ oz/3 tbsp caster (superfine) sugar

2.5 ml/¹/₂ tsp salt

350 g/12 oz/3 cups white gluten-free flour mix (see pages 11 and 12)

15 ml/1 tbsp xanthum gum

2.5 ml/¹/₂ tsp gluten-free mixed (apple pie) spice

1 sachet of easy-blend dried yeast

100 g/4 oz/²/₃ cup sultanas (golden raisins)

25 g/1 oz/3 tbsp glacé (candied) cherries, chopped

25 g/1 oz/3 tbsp chopped mixed (candied) peel

50 g/2 oz/¹/₂ cup chopped almonds

A little oil for greasing

225 g/8 oz white marzipan

A little icing (confectioners') sugar for dusting

1 Beat together the egg and milk, then pour into the breadmaker pan. Add the melted butter, sugar and salt.

2 Mix together the flour, gum and spice, then tip into the pan. Finally, sprinkle the yeast on top.

3 Set the machine to Dough. Run the machine for 17 minutes, then add the fruit, peel and nuts. Continue to run the machine until the dough has kneaded but has not started to heat and rise (about another 3 minutes, depending on the model).

4 Meanwhile, take a double-thickness sheet of heavy-duty foil and shape it into an oval boat shape, about 23 cm/ 9 in long, 13 cm/5 in wide and 7.5 cm/3 in deep. Brush inside with oil and place on a baking (cookie) sheet.

5 Spoon half the mixture into the foil container.

6 Roll out the marzipan to a similar sized oval and lay on top of the mixture. Cover with the remaining batter.

7 Cover loosely with oiled clingfilm (plastic wrap) and leave to prove in a warm place for about 45 minutes until doubled in size.

8 Meanwhile, preheat the oven to 190°C/375°F/gas 5/fan oven 170°C.

9 Bake for about 40 minutes until golden and cooked through. Allow to cool slightly, then remove from the foil and transfer to a wire rack. Dust with icing sugar and leave to cool completely.

Simple cornbread

This bread is popular in America, where it is served with any savoury dish. Enjoy it warm or cold with everything from a spicy chilli con carne to a traditional chicken casserole.

MAKES 1 MEDIUM LOAF

3 eggs

300 ml/½ pt/1¼ cups milk

10 ml/2 tsp lemon juice

175 g/6 oz/¾ cup white vegetable fat (shortening), melted

250 g/9 oz/2¼ cups maize flour

7.5 ml/1½ tsp salt

15 ml/1 tbsp gluten-free baking powder

1 Beat together the eggs, milk and lemon juice, then pour into the breadmaker pan. Add the melted fat.

2 Add the remaining ingredients.

3 Set the machine to Dough and run the machine for 5 minutes only, scraping down the sides twice, until the mixture is smooth. Switch off the machine. Remove the paddle.

4 Set the machine to Bake Only or Extrabake. Bake for about 50 minutes until risen and firm to the touch.

5 When cooked, turn off the machine and leave the bread in it for 15 minutes, then turn out on to a wire rack.

6 Serve warm, cut into squares.

Tea Breads

Tea breads are wonderful when eaten still warm, spread with butter or margarine. They are also delicious toasted when they get a little staler. They all freeze well, too, or can be refreshed by heating briefly in the microwave or in a low oven for 5 minutes.

If your breadmaker has a fruit and nut dispenser, add the fruit or nuts in this and they will be added to the dough at the appropriate time. If you have an older machine that doesn't have any facility for adding 'extras', tip them in after the first knead. If the recipe uses wet or sticky fruits, it is better to add them manually rather than through a dispenser.

You will see that for some I have used xanthum gum to give a good elastic texture. You can omit it for more cakey-textured loaves (more like ones made with baking powder), if you prefer. Experiment to see which you like best.

Blueberry tea bread

The blackcurrant cordial in this delicious loaf really brings out the flavour of the blueberries. If you don't have any, substitute 30 ml/2 tbsp clear honey and 30 ml/2 tbsp water instead.

MAKES 1 MEDIUM LOAF

75 g/3 oz/½ cup dried blueberries

75 ml/5 tbsp milk

2 eggs

175 ml/6 fl oz/¾ cup plain yoghurt

50 g/2 oz/¼ cup butter or margarine, melted

60 ml/4 tbsp blackcurrant cordial

5 ml/1 tsp lemon juice

275 g/10 oz/2½ cups white gluten-free flour mix (see pages 11 and 12)

45 ml/3 tbsp dried milk powder (non-fat dry milk)

40 g/1½ oz/3 tbsp caster (superfine) sugar

10 ml/2 tsp xanthum gum

2.5 ml/½ tsp salt

2.5 ml/½ tsp bicarbonate of soda (baking soda)

1 sachet of easy-blend dried yeast

1 Soak the blueberries in the milk for 30 minutes.

2 Drain off the milk into a bowl and whisk in the eggs and yoghurt. Pour into the breadmaker pan and add the melted butter or margarine, blackcurrant cordial and lemon juice.

3 Mix together the flour, milk powder, sugar, gum, salt and bicarbonate of soda, then tip into the pan.

4 Finally, sprinkle the yeast on top.

5 Set the machine to Basic, 700 g/1½ lb/Medium, light or medium crust.

6 Add the blueberries when the ten beeps sound after the first knead.

7 When cooked, leave to cool in the breadmaker for 10 minutes, then turn out on to a wire rack. When cool enough to handle, remove the paddle, if necessary.

8 Eat warm or cold within four days or slice and freeze.

Minted currant loaf

The flavour of mint blends beautifully with the currants in this delicious tea bread. You can serve it with tea or as a snack. It's also very good toasted for breakfast.

MAKES 1 MEDIUM LOAF

2 eggs

250 ml/8 fl oz/1 cup milk

5 ml/1 tsp distilled white vinegar

50 g/2 oz/¼ cup butter or margarine, melted

45 ml/3 tbsp clear honey

40 g/1½ oz/3 tbsp caster (superfine) sugar

175 g/6 oz/1½ cups brown rice flour

50 g/2 oz/½ cup potato flour

50 g/2 oz/½ cup tapioca flour

10 ml/2 tsp xanthum gum

2.5 ml/½ tsp salt

2.5 ml/½ tsp bicarbonate of soda (baking soda)

10 ml/2 tsp dried mint

1 sachet of easy-blend dried yeast

100 g/4 oz/⅔ cup currants

1 Beat together the eggs and milk, then pour into the breadmaker pan. Add the vinegar, melted butter or margarine, honey and sugar.

2 Mix together the flours, gum, salt, bicarbonate of soda and mint, then tip into the pan.

3 Finally, sprinkle the yeast on top.

4 Set the machine to Basic, 700 g/1½ lb/Medium, light or medium crust.

5 Add the currants when the 10 beeps sound after the first knead.

6 When cooked, switch off the machine and leave the bread to cool in the breadmaker for 10 minutes. When cool enough to handle, remove the paddle, if necessary.

7 Eat warm or cold within four days or slice and freeze.

Cinnamon raisin loaf

If you use a fruit and nut dispenser, if your breadmaker has one, make sure the apples are well mixed with the raisins so they don't stick to the lid, otherwise they won't get into your bread!

2 eggs

250 ml/8 fl oz/1 cup apple juice

50 g/2 oz/¼ cup butter or margarine, melted

5 ml/1 tsp cider vinegar

50 g/2 oz/¼ cup demerara sugar

225 g/8 oz/2 cups white rice flour

50 g/2 oz/½ cup potato flour

10 ml/2 tsp xanthum gum

5 ml/1 tsp ground cinnamon

2.5 ml/½ tsp salt

2.5 ml/½ tsp bicarbonate of soda (baking soda)

1 sachet of easy-blend dried yeast

2 eating (dessert) apples, peeled and finely chopped

50 g/2 oz/⅓ cup raisins

1   Beat together the eggs and apple juice, then pour into the breadmaker pan. Add the melted butter or margarine, the vinegar and 40 g/1½ oz/3 tbsp of the sugar.

2   Mix together the flours, gum, cinnamon, salt and bicarbonate of soda. Tip into the pan and sprinkle the yeast over.

3   Set the machine to Basic, 700 g/1½ lb/Medium, light or medium crust.

4   Add the chopped apple and raisins when the 10 beeps sound after the first knead.

5   50 minutes before the end of the programme, gently open the lid as little as possible and quickly sprinkle the top with the remaining sugar. Gently close the lid again.

6   When cooked, switch off the machine and leave the bread to cool in the breadmaker for 10 minutes. Turn out on to a wire rack. When cool enough to handle, remove the paddle, if necessary.

7   Eat warm or cold within four days or slice and freeze.

Spiced fruit bread

*If you prefer, you can use all raisins instead of the
dried mixed fruit. The recipe is also good if you
use cinnamon instead of the mixed spice.
Never be afraid to experiment!*

MAKES 1 MEDIUM LOAF

1 egg

60 ml/4 tbsp milk

284 ml/9 fl oz/1 carton of
buttermilk

50 g/2 oz/¼ cup butter or
margarine, melted

350 g/12 oz/3 cups white gluten-
free flour mix (see pages 11
and 12)

5 ml/1 tsp gluten-free mixed
(apple pie) spice

75 g/3 oz/⅓ cup light brown
sugar

10 ml/2 tsp xanthum gum

5 ml/1 tsp salt

2.5 ml/½ tsp bicarbonate of soda
(baking soda)

1 sachet of easy-blend dried yeast

100 g/4 oz/⅔ cup dried mixed
fruit (fruit cake mix)

1 Beat together the egg, milk and buttermilk, then pour
   into the breadmaker pan. Add the melted butter or
   margarine.

2 Mix together the flour, spice, sugar, gum, salt and
   bicarbonate of soda and add to the pan. Sprinkle the
   yeast on top.

3 Set the machine to Basic, 700 g/1½ lb/Medium, light or
   medium crust.

4 Add the fruit when the ten beeps sound after the first
   knead.

5 When cooked, leave in the breadmaker for 10 minutes,
   then turn the loaf out on to a wire rack. When cool
   enough to handle, remove the paddle, if necessary.

6 Eat warm or cold within four days or slice and freeze.

Chocolate mallow loaf

Try this spread with gluten-free chocolate hazelnut spread for self-indulgence personified! There's too many 'extras' to put in a fruit and nut dispenser, so add them after the first knead if you don't have beeps.

MAKES 1 MEDIUM LOAF

3 eggs

325 ml/11 fl oz /scant 1⅓ cups water

5 ml/1 tsp lemon juice

50 g/2 oz/¼ cup butter or margarine, melted

350 g/12 oz/3 cups brown gluten-free flour mix (see pages 11 and 12)

10 ml/2 tsp xanthum gum

45 ml/3 tbsp cocoa (unsweetened chocolate) powder

45 ml/3 tbsp dried milk powder (non-fat dry milk)

2.5 ml/½ tsp salt

2.5 ml/½ tsp bicarbonate of soda (baking soda)

100 g/4 oz/½ cup light brown sugar

1 sachet of easy-blend dried yeast

50 g/2 oz/⅓ cup baby marshmallows

50 g/2 oz/⅓ cup raisins

50 g/2 oz/½ cup chocolate chips

1 Beat together the eggs and water, then pour into the breadmaker pan. Add the lemon juice and melted butter or margarine.

2 Sift together the flour, gum and cocoa, then tip into the pan. Add the milk powder, salt, bicarbonate of soda and sugar.

3 Finally, sprinkle the yeast on top.

4 Set the machine to Basic, 700 g/1½ lb/Medium, light or medium crust.

5 Add the marshmallows, raisins and chocolate chips when the 10 beeps sound after the first knead.

6 When cooked, leave to cool in the breadmaker for 10 minutes, then turn out on to a wire rack.

7 When cool enough to handle, remove the paddle, if necessary.

8 Eat warm or cold within four days, or slice and freeze.

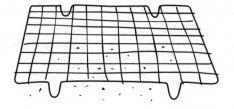

Cinnamon loaf

This is a sweet, delicately flavoured loaf with a nice nutty texture. When stale you can use it for bread and butter pudding – the added flavours of almonds and cinnamon make it especially delicious.

MAKES 1 MEDIUM LOAF

2 eggs

250 ml/8 fl oz/1 cup milk

65 g/2½ oz/generous ¼ cup butter or margarine, melted

5 ml/1 tsp lemon juice

175 g/6 oz/1½ cups white rice flour

100 g/4 oz/1 cup potato flour

50 g/2 oz/½ cup soya flour

2.5 ml/½ tsp salt

2.5 ml/½ tsp bicarbonate of soda (baking soda)

10 ml/2 tsp xanthum gum

75 g/3 oz/⅓ cup light brown sugar

50 g/2 oz/½ cup ground almonds

7.5 ml/1½ tsp ground cinnamon

1 sachet of easy-blend dried yeast

50 g/2 oz/½ cup chopped blanched almonds or mixed nuts

1 Beat together the eggs and milk, then pour into the breadmaker pan.

2 Add 50 g/2 oz/¼ cup of the melted butter or margarine and the lemon juice.

3 Mix together the flours, salt, bicarbonate of soda, gum, sugar, ground almonds and cinnamon, then tip into the pan.

4 Sprinkle the yeast on top.

5 Set the machine to Basic, 700 g/1½ lb/Medium, light or medium crust.

6 Add the chopped nuts when the 10 beeps sound after the first knead.

7 When cooked, leave to cool in the breadmaker for 10 minutes, then turn the loaf out on to a wire rack and brush all over with the remaining melted butter. When cool enough to handle, remove the paddle, if necessary.

8 Eat warm or cold within four days or slice and freeze.

Moist hazelnut bread

As the name suggests, this makes a deliciously moist tea bread. It is lovely spread with butter and raspberry jam for a real teatime treat.

MAKES 1 MEDIUM LOAF

2 eggs

175 ml/6 fl oz/³/₄ cup plain yoghurt

75 ml/5 tbsp milk

50 g/2 oz/¹/₄ cup butter or margarine, melted

60 ml/4 tbsp clear honey

5 ml/1 tsp lemon juice

25 g/1 oz/2 tbsp light brown sugar

275 g/10 oz/2¹/₂ cups brown gluten-free flour mix (see pages 11 and 12)

45 ml/3 tbsp dried milk powder (non-fat dry milk)

10 ml/2 tsp xanthum gum

2.5 ml/¹/₂ tsp salt

2.5 ml/¹/₂ tsp bicarbonate of soda (baking soda)

1 sachet of easy-blend dried yeast

100 g/4 oz/1 cup chopped hazelnuts (filberts)

1 Whisk the eggs with the yoghurt and milk and tip into the breadmaker pan.

2 Add the melted butter or margarine, honey, lemon juice and sugar.

3 Mix together the flour, milk powder, gum, salt and bicarbonate of soda, then tip into the pan.

4 Sprinkle the yeast on top.

5 Set the machine to Basic, 700 g/1¹/₂ lb/Medium, light or medium crust.

6 Add the nuts when the 10 beeps sound after the first knead.

7 When cooked, leave to cool in the breadmaker for 10 minutes, then turn out on to a wire rack and remove the paddle, if necessary. Leave to cool completely.

8 Eat warm or cold within four days or slice and freeze.

Banana bread

*Banana bread is usually made with baking powder, but
I find yeast loaves so much better in the breadmaker.
This one has a delicious moist texture and is the ideal
way to use up overripe fruit.*

MAKES 1 MEDIUM LOAF

1 large egg

300 ml/½ pt /1¼ cups water

30 ml/2 tbsp sunflower oil

30 ml/2 tbsp dried milk powder
(non-fat dry milk)

100 g/4 oz/½ cup caster
(superfine) sugar

2 small or 1 large ripe banana,
mashed

400 g/14 oz/3½ cups white
gluten-free flour mix (see pages
11 and 12)

7.5 ml/1½ tsp xanthum gum

5 ml/1 tsp gluten-free mixed
(apple pie) spice

2.5 ml/½ tsp salt

2.5 ml/½ tsp bicarbonate of soda
(baking soda)

1 sachet of easy-blend dried yeast

1 Beat together the eggs and water, then pour into the
breadmaker pan.

2 Add the oil, milk powder, sugar and banana.

3 Mix together the flour, gum, spice, salt and bicarbonate
of soda, then tip into the pan.

4 Finally, sprinkle the yeast on top.

5 Set the machine to Basic, 700 g/1½ lb/Medium, light or
medium crust.

6 When cooked, leave in the breadmaker for 10 minutes,
then turn out on to a wire rack. When cool enough to
handle, remove the paddle, if necessary. Leave to cool
completely.

7 Eat warm or cold within four days or slice and freeze.

Banana cherry bread

Glacé cherries add colour and texture to the loaf. You can make a more exotic one by using some of the moist preserved fruits, such as forest fruits or wild berries, available in the supermarket, instead of cherries.

MAKES 1 MEDIUM LOAF

1 large egg

300 ml/¹/₂ pt/1¹/₄ cups water

30 ml/2 tbsp sunflower oil

30 ml/2 tbsp dried milk powder (non-fat dry milk)

100 g/4 oz/¹/₂ cup light brown sugar

2 small or 1 large ripe banana, mashed

400 g/14 oz/3¹/₂ cups white gluten-free flour mix (see pages 11 and 12)

7.5 ml/1¹/₂ tsp xanthum gum

5 ml/1 tsp ground cinnamon

2.5 ml/¹/₂ tsp salt

2.5 ml/¹/₂ tsp bicarbonate of soda (baking soda)

1 sachet of easy-blend dried yeast

75 g/3 oz/¹/₃ cup glacé (candied) cherries, roughly chopped

1 Beat together the egg and water, then pour into the breadmaker pan.

2 Add the oil, milk powder, sugar and banana.

3 Mix together the flour, gum, cinnamon, salt and bicarbonate of soda, then tip into the pan.

4 Finally, sprinkle the yeast on top.

5 Set the machine to Basic, 700 g/1¹/₂ lb/Medium, light or medium crust.

6 Add the cherries when the 10 beeps sound after the first knead.

7 When cooked, leave in the breadmaker for 10 minutes, then turn out on to a wire rack. When cool enough to handle, remove the paddle, if necessary.

8 Eat warm or cold within four days or slice and freeze.

Cranberry orange bread

This loaf makes the most of the popular combination of cranberry and orange. I also like to make it with the grated zest and juice of a lime instead of an orange for a change.

MAKES 1 MEDIUM LOAF

2 eggs

30 ml/2 tbsp water

175 ml/6 fl oz/³⁄₄ cup plain yoghurt

Finely grated zest and juice of 1 orange

45 ml/3 tbsp clear honey

50 g/2 oz/¹⁄₄ cup butter or margarine, melted

40 ml/1¹⁄₂ oz/3 tbsp caster (superfine) sugar

275 g/10 oz/2¹⁄₂ cups white gluten-free flour mix (see pages 11 and 12)

10 ml/2 tsp xanthum gum

2.5 ml/¹⁄₂ tsp salt

2.5 ml/¹⁄₂ tsp bicarbonate of soda (baking soda)

1 sachet of easy-blend dried yeast

75 g/3 oz/¹⁄₂ cup dried cranberries

1 Beat together eggs, water and yoghurt, then tip into the breadmaker pan.

2 Add the orange zest and juice, honey, melted butter or margarine and sugar.

3 Mix together the flour, gum, salt and bicarbonate of soda then tip into the pan.

4 Sprinkle the yeast on top.

5 Set the machine to Basic, 700 g/1¹⁄₂ lb/Medium, light or medium crust.

6 Add the cranberries when the 10 beeps sound after the first knead.

7 When cooked, leave in the breadmaker for 10 minutes, then turn out on to a wire rack. When cool enough to handle, remove the paddle, if necessary.

8 Eat warm or cold within four days or slice and freeze.

Shaped Breads and Buns

~

In this section, you'll find you can really broaden your horizons. Using the dough programme to do the hard work, you can then shape and bake all kinds of buns and different-style breads.

Soft white pitta breads

This recipe makes soft, light breads that are even better than wheat flour ones, which can sometimes be tough and dry. Serve them cut into strips with dips or split them and fill with salad or other fillings.

MAKES 8

1 egg

120 ml/4 fl oz/¹/₂ cup warm milk

30 ml/2 tbsp sunflower oil

100 ml/3¹/₂ fl oz/scant ¹/₂ cup plain yoghurt

350 g/12 oz/3 cups white gluten-free flour mix (see pages 11 and 12), plus extra for dusting

10 ml/2 tsp caster (superfine) sugar

4 ml/³/₄ tsp salt

2.5 ml/¹/₂ tsp gluten-free baking powder

10 ml/2 tsp easy-blend dried yeast

1 Beat together the egg, milk, oil and yoghurt, then pour into the breadmaker.

2 Add the remaining ingredients in the order listed.

3 Set the machine to Dough.

4 When the dough has kneaded and proved, turn it out on to a board dusted with a little extra gluten-free flour.

5 Preheat the oven to as hot as possible and place a baking (cookie) sheet in to heat.

6 Shape the dough into eight balls. Roll each into an oval pitta bread shape about 5 mm/¹/₄ in thick, covering the dough and the shaped pittas quickly with a damp cloth to prevent drying out while making the remainder.

7 When hot, transfer the pittas to the baking sheet, using a fish slice and bake for 3 minutes until puffy but still pale.

8 Either eat while still warm or wrap in a clean cloth and leave to cool, then freeze. Reheat in a toaster, under the grill (broiler) or in the microwave before eating.

Sesame pitta breads

These are great cut into strips to serve with dips such as hummus or taramasalata or split and filled with any mixtures of your choice. If you don't have any sesame oil, increase the sunflower oil instead.

MAKES 8

1 egg

120 ml/4 fl oz/½ cup warm milk

30 ml/2 tbsp sunflower oil

100 ml/3½ fl oz/scant ½ cup plain yoghurt

350 g/12 oz/3 cups brown gluten-free flour mix (see pages 11 and 12), plus extra for dusting

10 ml/2 tsp caster (superfine) sugar

4 ml/¾ tsp salt

2.5 ml/½ tsp gluten-free baking powder

10 ml/2 tsp easy-blend dried yeast

30 ml/2 tbsp sesame seeds

15 ml/1 tbsp sesame oil

1 Beat together the egg, milk, oil and yoghurt, then pour into the breadmaker. Add the remaining ingredients in the order listed except the sesame seeds and oil.

2 Set the machine to Dough.

3 When the dough has kneaded and proved, turn it out on to a board dusted with a little extra gluten-free flour.

4 Preheat the oven to as hot as possible and place a baking (cookie) sheet in to heat.

5 Shape the dough into eight balls and sprinkle each with sesame seeds. Roll each into an oval pitta bread shape about 5 mm/¼ in thick, covering the dough and the shaped pittas quickly with a damp cloth to prevent drying out while making the remainder.

6 When hot, transfer the pittas to the baking sheet and brush quickly with the sesame oil. Bake for 3 minutes until puffy but still pale.

7 Either eat while still warm or wrap in a clean cloth and leave to cool, then freeze. Reheat in a toaster, under the grill (broiler) or in the microwave before eating.

Breadsticks

If you prefer your breadsticks to be soft in the centre and crisp on the outside, roll the dough slightly thicker and bake for 15 minutes instead of the 20 minutes in the method.

MAKES 24

175 ml/6 fl oz/³/₄ cup water

30 ml/2 tbsp olive oil, plus extra for greasing

175 g/6 oz/1¹/₂ cups white or brown rice flour

50 g/2 oz/¹/₂ cup tapioca flour

100 g/4 oz/1 cup potato flour

15 g/¹/₂ oz/2 tbsp cornflour (cornstarch), plus extra for dusting

10 ml/2 tsp xanthum gum

4 ml/³/₄ tsp salt

10 ml/2 tsp sugar

10 ml/2 tsp easy-blend dried yeast

1 small egg, beaten

1 Pour the water and oil into the breadmaker pan. Add the flours, gum, salt and sugar.

2 Finally, sprinkle the yeast on top.

3 Set the machine to Dough.

4 When the dough has kneaded and proved, tip it out on to a work surface dusted with cornflour. Divide it into 24 equal pieces and roll each one into a long stick about the width of a little finger.

5 Oil a baking (cookie) sheet and transfer the breadsticks to it. Brush with the beaten egg to glaze. Cover loosely with oiled clingfilm (plastic wrap) and leave in a warm place for 15 minutes to rest and rise slightly.

6 Meanwhile, preheat the oven to 220°C/425°F/gas 7/fan oven 200°C.

7 Bake the breadsticks for about 20 minutes until crisp and golden. Transfer to a wire rack to cool.

8 Best eaten fresh, or store in an airtight container and refresh by heating briefly in the oven or microwave.

Spiced flat breads

These breads can be frozen and then reheated briefly either in the toaster, under the grill or in the microwave. Try adding a handful of chopped fresh coriander to the dough for added flavour and colour.

MAKES 8

175 ml/6 fl oz/³/₄ cup warm but not hot water

30 ml/2 tbsp olive oil, plus extra for brushing

100 g/4 oz/1 cup white rice flour

100 g/4 oz/1 cup gram flour

25 g/1 oz/¹/₄ cup cornflour (cornstarch), plus extra for dusting

5 ml/1 tsp ground cumin

10 ml/2 tsp cumin seeds

2.5 ml/¹/₂ tsp salt

5 ml/1 tsp caster (superfine) sugar

10 ml/2 tsp xanthum gum

10 ml/2 tsp easy-blend dried yeast

1 Pour the water and oil into the breadmaker pan.

2 Mix together the flours, cumin, salt, sugar and gum, then tip into the pan.

3 Finally, sprinkle the yeast on top.

4 Set the machine to Dough.

5 When the dough has kneaded but has not yet started to heat and rise (about 20 minutes, depending on the model), tip it out on to a work surface dusted with cornflour.

6 Shape the dough into eight balls. Flatten each to a round, about 12 cm/4¹/₂ in diameter.

7 Transfer the breads to a sheet of non-stick baking parchment on a baking (cookie) sheet. Cover with a damp cloth and leave in a warm place for about 30 minutes to rise slightly.

8 Lightly oil a heavy frying pan (skillet). Add the breads, two at a time, and cook gently for 2–3 minutes until lightly golden underneath and puffing up slightly.

9 Turn over and cook for about 2 minutes until the breads are cooked through. Wrap in a clean cloth while cooking the remainder. Serve warm.

Cheese and onion breads

*These are really moreish for a snack on their own but are
also great served with soup to make a filling lunch or
supper dish. You can also serve them as an accompaniment
to grilled meat, chicken or fish.*

MAKES 8

1 egg

120 ml/4 fl oz/½ cup milk

60 ml/4 tbsp olive oil

100 ml/3½ fl oz/scant ½ cup
plain yoghurt

350 g/12 oz/3 cups white gluten-
free flour mix (see pages 11
and 12)

10 ml/2 tsp caster (superfine)
sugar

4 ml/¾ tsp salt

2.5 ml/½ tsp gluten-free baking
powder

10 ml/2 tsp easy-blend dried
yeast

2 onions, thinly sliced

15 ml/1 tbsp chopped fresh
thyme

15 ml/1 tbsp chopped fresh sage

15 ml/1 tbsp chopped fresh
parsley

100 g/4 oz/1 cup grated Cheddar
cheese

Freshly ground black pepper

1 Beat together the egg, milk, 30 ml/2 tbsp of the oil and
the yoghurt, then pour into the breadmaker pan.

2 Mix together the flour, sugar, salt and baking powder
and tip into the pan.

3 Finally, sprinkle the yeast on top.

4 Set the machine to Dough.

5 When the dough has kneaded and proved, tip it out on to
a surface dusted with a little gluten-free flour. Divide into
eight balls and roll out each to a round, about 5 mm/¼ in
thick, covering the dough and the shaped breads quickly
with a damp cloth to prevent drying out while making
the remainder.

6 Meanwhile, preheat the oven to as hot as possible. Put a
baking (cookie) sheet in to heat.

7　Transfer the breads to the hot baking sheet. Bake in the oven for 3 minutes only until puffy but still pale. Remove from the oven.

8　Meanwhile, fry (sauté) the onions in half the remaining oil for 3 minutes, stirring, until softened but not browned.

9　Brush the rounds with the remaining oil and spread the onion slices over the tops. Sprinkle with the herbs and cheese and add a sprinkling of salt and a good grinding of pepper to each.

10 Bake in the oven for about 5 minutes until the cheese melts and bubbles. Serve warm.

Salt and herb rolls

These are delicious served warm with hot soup or as an accompaniment to starters, particularly pâtés or delicatessen meat platters.

MAKES 10

2 eggs

200 ml/7 fl oz/scant 1 cup warm but not hot water

5 ml/1 tsp lemon juice

60 ml/4 tbsp sunflower oil, plus extra for greasing

45 ml/3 tbsp dried milk powder (non-fat dry milk)

225 g/8 oz/2 cups white rice flour

50 g/2 oz/¹/₂ cup tapioca flour

50 g/2 oz/¹/₂ cup potato flour

15 ml/1 tbsp xanthum gum

30 ml/2 tbsp snipped fresh chives or 10 ml/2 tsp dried

7.5 ml/1¹/₂ tsp salt

20 ml/1¹/₂ tbsp caster (superfine) sugar

1 sachet of easy-blend dried yeast

15 ml/1 tbsp single (light) or double (heavy) cream

15 ml/1 tbsp coarse sea salt

5 ml/1 tsp Herbes de Provence

1 Beat together the eggs, water, lemon juice, oil and milk powder. Tip into the breadmaker pan.

2 Add the flours, gum, chives, salt and sugar.

3 Finally, sprinkle the yeast on top.

4 Set the machine to Dough.

5 When the dough has kneaded and proved, turn it into a piping (pastry) bag with a large plain tube (tip) or a plastic bag with the corner cut off. Pipe the dough into 10 sausage shapes, well apart on a greased baking (cookie) sheet. Cover loosely with oiled clingfilm (plastic wrap) and leave in a warm place for about 40 minutes or until doubled in size.

6 Meanwhile, preheat the oven to 200°C/400°F/gas 6/fan oven 180°C.

7 Remove the clingfilm and brush the dough lightly with the cream. Mix together the salt and herbs and sprinkle over.

8 Bake in the oven for about 25 minutes or until golden and cooked through. The rolls should sound hollow when tapped on the base. Transfer to a wire rack and cover with a damp tea towel to soften the crusts.

9 Serve warm or cold.

Floury milk buns

*These little savoury buns have a delicious aroma
and flavour. They can be served with any meal
but are especially good for breakfast.*

MAKES 10

1 large egg, beaten

275 ml/9 fl oz/scant 1¼ cups
warm but not hot milk

30 ml/2 tbsp sunflower oil, plus
extra for greasing

4 ml/¾ tsp salt

15 ml/1 tbsp caster (superfine)
sugar

225 g/8 oz/2 cups white rice
flour

10 ml/2 tsp xanthum gum

1 sachet of easy-blend dried yeast

15 ml/1 tbsp cornflour
(cornstarch) for dusting

1   Reserve about a quarter of the egg for glazing and beat
    the rest with the milk. Pour into the breadmaker pan.

2   Add all the remaining ingredients in the order listed.

3   Set the machine to Dough.

4   When the dough has kneaded but has not yet started to
    heat and rise (about 20 minutes, depending on the
    model), switch off the breadmaker.

5   Oil 10 sections of a tartlet tin (pan) and dust with
    cornflour (cornstarch). Spoon the dough into the pans.
    Using oiled hands, neatly round off the tops. Cover
    loosely with oiled clingfilm (plastic wrap) and leave in a
    warm place for about 45 minutes or until doubled in
    size.

6   Meanwhile, preheat the oven to 200°C/400°F/gas 6/fan
    oven 180°C.

7   Remove the clingfilm and brush the tops of the dough
    very gently with the reserved beaten egg, then dust with
    the cornflour.

8 Bake in the oven for about 25 minutes until golden and the bases sound hollow when removed from the tin and tapped.

9 These buns are best eaten warm and they can also be frozen.

Finger rolls

If you want to use these for hot dogs, make eight slightly longer rolls instead of ten short ones. You can use them with frankfurters or ordinary sausages.

MAKES 10

2 eggs

250 ml/8 fl oz/1 cup warm but not hot water

5 ml/1 tsp lemon juice

60 ml/4 tbsp sunflower oil

45 ml/3 tbsp dried milk powder (non-fat dry milk)

225 g/8 oz/2 cups white rice flour

50 g/2 oz/$^1/_2$ cup tapioca flour

50 g/2 oz/$^1/_2$ cup potato flour

15 ml/1 tbsp xanthum gum

7.5 ml/1$^1/_2$ tsp salt

20 ml/1$^1/_2$ tbsp caster (superfine) sugar

1 sachet of easy-blend dried yeast

A little milk for glazing

1 Beat together the eggs, water and lemon juice, then pour into the breadmaker pan.

2 Add the remaining ingredients in the order listed.

3 Set the machine to Dough.

4 When the mixture has kneaded and proved, turn it into a piping (pastry) bag with a large plain tube (tip) or a plastic bag with the corner cut off. Pipe the dough into 10 sausage shapes, well apart on a greased baking (cookie) sheet. Cover loosely with oiled clingfilm (plastic wrap) and leave in a warm place for about 40 minutes or until doubled in size.

5 Meanwhile, preheat the oven to 200°C/400°F/gas 6/fan oven 180°C.

6 Remove the clingfilm and brush the dough lightly with milk to glaze.

7 Bake in the oven for about 25 minutes or until golden and cooked through. The rolls should sound hollow when tapped on the base. Transfer to a wire rack and cover with a damp tea towel to soften the crusts.

8 Best served warm. Can be frozen.

Seeded burger buns

These buns mean you don't have to go without your burgers-in-a-bun any more. Pipe the dough into eight slightly larger buns if you eat quarter pounders!

MAKES 10

2 eggs

200 ml/7 fl oz/scant 1 cup warm but not hot water

5 ml/1 tsp lemon juice

50 g/2 oz/¼ cup butter or margarine, melted

45 ml/3 tbsp dried milk powder (non-fat dry milk)

225 g/8 oz/2 cups white rice flour

50 g/2 oz/½ cup tapioca flour

50 g/2 oz/½ cup potato flour

15 ml/1 tbsp xanthum gum

7.5 ml/1½ tsp salt

20 ml/1½ tbsp caster (superfine) sugar

1 sachet of easy-blend dried yeast

A little milk for glazing

30 ml/2 tbsp sesame seeds

1 Beat together the eggs, water and lemon juice, then pour into the breadmaker pan.

2 Add the remaining ingredients except the milk and sesame seeds in the order listed.

3 Set the machine to Dough.

4 When the mixture has kneaded and proved, turn it into a piping (pastry) bag with a large plain tube (tip) or a plastic bag with the corner cut off. Pipe the dough into 10 balls well apart on a greased baking (cookie) sheet. With oiled hands, flatten the balls slightly. Cover loosely with oiled clingfilm (plastic wrap) and leave in a warm place for about 40 minutes or until doubled in size.

5 Meanwhile, preheat the oven to 200°C/400°F/gas 6/fan oven 180°C.

6 Remove the clingfilm and brush the dough lightly with milk, then sprinkle with the sesame seeds.

7   Bake in the oven for about 25 minutes or until golden and cooked through. The rolls should sound hollow when tapped on the base. Transfer to a wire rack and cover with a damp tea towel to soften the crusts.

8   Best served warm. Can be frozen.

Savoury pine nut whirls

*Experiment with other flavoured cheeses like
soft cheese with chives or with black pepper,
and try pumpkin or sunflower seeds instead
of pine nuts for a change.*

MAKES 9

1 egg

275 ml/9 fl oz/scant 1¼ cups
warm but not hot milk

50 g/2 oz/¼ cup butter or
margarine, melted

350 g/12 oz/3 cups white gluten-
free flour mix (see pages 11
and 12)

15 ml/1 tbsp xanthum gum

7.5 ml/1½ tsp salt

20 ml/1½ tbsp caster (superfine)
sugar

1 sachet of easy-blend dried yeast

A little oil for greasing

200 g/7 oz/scant 1 cup garlic
and herb soft cheese

30 ml/2 tbsp cold milk

50 g/2 oz/½ cup pine nuts

1   Whisk together the egg and warm milk, then pour into
the breadmaker pan.

2   Add 40 g/1½ oz/3 tbsp of the melted butter or
margarine, then the flour, gum, salt and sugar.

3   Finally, sprinkle the yeast on top.

4   Set the machine to Dough.

5   When the dough has kneaded but has not started to heat
and rise (about 20 minutes depending on the model),
switch off the machine.

6   Turn out the dough on to a sheet of oiled greaseproof
(waxed) paper. Place another oiled sheet on top, oiled-
side down, and roll the dough out to a rectangle about
23 cm/9 in by 30 cm/12 in.

7   Blend the cheese with the cold milk to soften it slightly.
Remove the top piece of greaseproof (waxed) paper and
gently spread the dough with the cheese. Sprinkle with
the pine nuts.

8 Roll up the dough using the second piece of greaseproof paper to help. Cut the roll into nine slices with a wet knife. Place the rolls about 5 mm/¼ in apart, cut-sides up, on an oiled baking (cookie) sheet in three rows of three buns to form a square. Cover loosely with oiled clingfilm (plastic wrap) and leave in a warm place for about 45 minutes until doubled in size and the buns are just sitting snugly side by side.

9 Meanwhile, preheat the oven to 200°C/400°F/gas 6/fan oven 180°C.

10 Remove the clingfilm and brush the buns with the remaining melted butter or margarine. Bake for about 25 minutes until golden and cooked through. Remove from the oven and transfer to a wire rack to cool. Best served warm. Can be frozen.

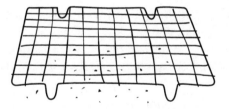

All-butter croissants

*You will love this recipe! I was delighted when
I managed to create gluten-free croissants for you to enjoy
for special breakfasts. They take a little effort but are
well worth it*

MAKES 8

For the dough:

1 egg

150 ml/¼ pt/⅔ cup warm but not hot milk

15 g/½ oz/1 tbsp butter, melted

4 ml/¾ tsp salt

15 ml/1 tbsp caster (superfine) sugar

225 g/8 oz/2 cups white gluten-free flour mix (see pages 11 and 12)

10 ml/2 tsp xanthum gum

1 sachet of easy-blend dried yeast

A little potato flour for dusting

50 g/2 oz/¼ cup hard butter

Oil for greasing

For the glaze:

1 egg yolk

2.5 ml/½ tsp caster sugar

15 ml/1 tbsp water

1 To make the dough, beat together the egg and milk, then pour into the breadmaker pan. Add the melted butter, salt, sugar, flour and gum. Finally, sprinkle the yeast on top.

2 Set the machine to Dough. When the dough has kneaded but has not yet started to heat and rise (about 20 minutes, depending on the model), switch off the machine.

3 Turn out the dough on to a work surface dusted with potato flour. Roll out the dough to an oblong about 1 cm/½ in thick.

4 Dot a third of the hard butter over the top two-thirds of the dough. Fold the undotted third up over, then the top third down over. Press gently with the rolling pin at the edges to seal and give the dough a quarter turn. Dust with a little more flour if necessary.

5 Repeat the rolling, dotting, folding and turning twice more, then put the dough in an oiled polythene bag and leave it to rest in the fridge for 30 minutes.

6 Roll and fold the dough twice more, without adding any more butter.

7 Roll out the dough to a large square, no thicker than 5 mm/¼ in, cut into four equal smaller squares, then cut each in half to form eight triangles.

8 To make the glaze, beat together the egg yolk, sugar and water and brush over the triangles. Starting from the long edge, roll the triangles up. Curve each roll into a crescent shape and place on a greased baking (cookie) sheet. Cover loosely with oiled clingfilm (plastic wrap) and leave in a warm place for about 45 minutes until doubled in size.

9 Meanwhile, preheat the oven to 200°C/400°F/gas 6/fan oven 180°C. Gently brush the croissants with a little more of the glaze, then bake in the oven for about 25 minutes until puffy and golden. Serve warm. Can be frozen.

Cheese croissants

*These are delicious warm either for breakfast or for lunch.
Try splitting them and adding a slice of ham or other cured
meat or some juicy, sliced tomatoes. Or you could sprinkle
them with cheese and flash them under the grill.*

MAKES 8

For the dough:

1 egg

150 ml/¹/₄ pt/²/₃ cup warm but not hot milk

15 g/¹/₂ oz/1 tbsp butter, melted

4 ml/³/₄ tsp salt

15 ml/1 tbsp caster (superfine) sugar

225 g/8 oz/2 cups white gluten-free flour mix (see pages 11 and 12)

10 ml/2 tsp xanthum gum

1 sachet of easy-blend dried yeast

A little potato flour for dusting

50 g/2 oz/¹/₄ cup hard butter

75 g/3 oz/³/₄ cup grated strong Cheddar cheese

Oil for greasing

For the glaze:

1 egg yolk

2.5 ml/¹/₂ tsp caster sugar

A pinch of salt

15 ml/1 tbsp water

1 To make the dough, beat together the egg and milk, then pour into the breadmaker pan. Add the melted butter, salt, sugar, flour and gum. Finally, sprinkle the yeast on top.

2 Set the machine to Dough. When the dough has kneaded but has not yet started to heat and rise (about 20 minutes, depending on the model), switch off the machine.

3 Turn out the dough on to a work surface dusted with potato flour. Roll out the dough to an oblong about 1 cm/¹/₂ in thick.

4 Dot a third of the hard butter over the top two-thirds of the dough. Sprinkle with a third of the cheese. Fold the undotted third up over, then the top third down over. Press gently with the rolling pin at the edges to seal and give the dough a quarter turn. Dust with a little more flour if necessary.

5 Repeat the rolling, dotting, sprinkling, folding and turning twice more, then put the dough in an oiled polythene bag and leave it to rest in the fridge for 30 minutes.

6 Roll and fold the dough twice more, without adding any more butter or cheese.

7 Roll out the dough to a large square, no thicker than 5 mm/¼ in, cut into four equal smaller squares, then cut each in half to form eight triangles.

8 To make the glaze, beat together the egg yolk, sugar, salt and water and brush over the triangles. Starting from the long edge, roll the triangles up. Curve each roll into a crescent shape and place on a greased baking (cookie) sheet. Cover loosely with oiled clingfilm (plastic wrap) and leave in a warm place for about 45 minutes until doubled in size.

9 Meanwhile, preheat the oven to 200°C/400°F/gas 6/fan oven 180°C. Gently brush the croissants with a little more of the glaze, then bake in the oven for about 25 minutes until puffy and golden. Serve warm. Can be frozen.

Pains au chocolat

Melting, chocolatey, heavenly buns, freshly squeezed orange juice and hot, strong coffee – a breakfast to die for! Now you no longer have to watch everyone else enjoying it – you can join in.

MAKES 8

For the dough:

1 egg

150 ml/¼ pt/⅔ cup warm but not hot milk

15 g/½ oz/1 tbsp butter, melted

4 ml/¾ tsp salt

15 ml/1 tbsp caster (superfine) sugar

225 g/8 oz/2 cups white gluten-free flour mix (see pages 11 and 12)

10 ml/2 tsp xanthum gum

1 sachet of easy-blend dried yeast

A little potato flour for dusting

50 g/2 oz/¼ cup hard butter

Oil for greasing

For the glaze and filling:

1 egg yolk

2.5 ml/½ tsp caster sugar

15 ml/1 tbsp water

24 squares of gluten-free chocolate

15 ml/1 tbsp icing (confectioners') sugar, sifted

1   To make the dough, beat together the egg and milk, then pour into the breadmaker pan. Add the melted butter, salt, sugar, flour and gum. Finally, sprinkle the yeast on top.

2   Set the machine to Dough. When the dough has kneaded but has not yet started to heat and rise (about 20 minutes, depending on the model), switch off the machine.

3   Turn out the dough on to a work surface dusted with potato flour. Roll out the dough to an oblong about 1 cm/½ in thick.

4   Dot a third of the hard butter over the top two-thirds of the dough. Fold the undotted third up over, then the top third down over. Press gently with the rolling pin at the edges to seal and give the dough a quarter turn. Dust with a little more flour if necessary.

5 Repeat the rolling, dotting, folding and turning twice more, then put the dough in an oiled polythene bag and leave it to rest in the fridge for 30 minutes.

6 Roll and fold the dough twice more, without adding any more butter.

7 Roll out the dough to a large rectangle no thicker than 5 mm/¼ in and cut into eight equal smaller squares.

8 To make the glaze, beat together the egg yolk, sugar, salt and water and brush over the squares. Place three squares of chocolate side-by-side in the centre of each square. Roll up the dough round the chocolate and place each roll on a greased baking (cookie) sheet. Cover loosely with oiled clingfilm (plastic wrap) and leave in a warm place for about 45 minutes until doubled in size.

9 Meanwhile, preheat the oven to 200°C/400°F/gas 6/fan oven 180°C. Gently brush the rolls with a little more of the glaze, then bake in the oven for about 25 minutes until puffy and golden. Dust with the icing sugar and serve warm. Can be frozen.

Pains au raisins

These were the nearest I could get to those melting, delicious buns you buy on every street corner in France. They are perfect for breakfast and also with a cup of tea in the afternoon.

MAKES 8

2 large eggs

150 ml/¼ pt/⅔ cup warm but not hot milk

15 g/½ oz/1 tbsp butter, melted

4 ml/¾ tsp salt

50 ml/3⅓ tbsp caster (superfine) sugar

225 g/8 oz/2 cups white gluten-free flour mix (see pages 11 and 12)

10 ml/2 tsp xanthum gum

1 sachet of easy-blend dried yeast

A little potato flour for dusting

50 g/2 oz/¼ cup hard butter

Oil for greasing

120 ml/4 fl oz/½ cup crème fraîche

75 g/3 oz/½ cup raisins

2.5 ml/½ tsp ground cinnamon

1 Beat together one of the eggs and the milk, then pour into the breadmaker pan. Add the melted butter, salt, 15 ml/1 tbsp of the sugar, the flour and gum. Finally, sprinkle the yeast on top.

2 Set the machine to Dough. When the dough has kneaded but has not yet started to heat and rise (about 20 minutes, depending on the model), switch off the machine.

3 Turn out the dough on to a work surface dusted with potato flour. Roll out the dough to an oblong about 1 cm/½ in thick.

4 Dot a third of the hard butter over the top two-thirds of the dough. Fold the undotted third up over, then the top third down over. Press gently with the rolling pin at the edges to seal and give the dough a quarter turn. Dust with a little more flour if necessary.

5 Repeat the rolling, dotting, folding and turning twice more, then put the dough in an oiled polythene bag and leave it to rest in the fridge for 30 minutes.

6 Roll and fold the dough twice more, without adding any more butter. Roll out the dough to a large oblong no thicker than 5 mm/¼ in and cut into eight equal smaller squares.

7 Beat the remaining egg, pour off about half of it and reserve. Beat the crème fraîche into one half with all but 5 ml/1 tsp of the remaining sugar. Stir in the raisins and cinnamon. Beat the remaining egg with the remaining sugar and brush over the surface of each square of dough.

8 Spoon the raisin mixture on the centre of each square. Draw the dough up over each, pinching the edges together, so only a little of the filling is visible and there are no gaps round the edges. Place on a greased baking (cookie) sheet, cover loosely with oiled clingfilm (plastic wrap) and leave in a warm place for about 45 minutes until doubled in size.

9 Meanwhile, preheat the oven to 200°C/400°F/gas 6/fan oven 180°C.

10 Bake in the oven for about 25 minutes until puffy and golden. Serve warm. Can be frozen.

Brie-filled french buns

These have to be served warm to enjoy their true texture and flavour. Ideally they should be eaten fresh but they can be reheated in a hot oven for a few minutes if you can't serve them straight away.

MAKES 8

For the dough:

1 egg

150 ml/¼ pt/⅔ cup warm but not hot milk

15 g/½ oz/1 tbsp butter, melted

4 ml/¾ tsp salt

15 ml/1 tbsp caster (superfine) sugar

225 g/8 oz/2 cups white gluten-free flour mix (see pages 11 and 12)

10 ml/2 tsp xanthum gum

1 sachet of easy-blend dried yeast

Potato flour for dusting

50 g/2 oz/¼ cup hard butter

Oil for greasing

For the glaze:

1 egg yolk

2.5 ml/½ tsp salt

15 ml/1 tbsp water

For the filling:

200 g/7 oz piece of Brie

10 ml/2 tsp Herbes de Provence

1 To make the dough, beat together the egg and milk, then pour into the breadmaker pan. Add the melted butter, salt, sugar, flour and gum. Finally, sprinkle the yeast on top.

2 Set the machine to Dough. When the dough has kneaded but has not yet started to heat and rise (about 20 minutes, depending on the model), switch off the machine.

3 Turn the dough out on to a surface dusted with potato flour. Roll out the dough to an oblong about 1 cm/½ in thick.

4 Dot a third of the hard butter over the top two-thirds of the dough. Fold the undotted third up over, then the top third down over. Press gently with the rolling pin at the edges to seal and give the dough a quarter turn. Dust with a little more flour if necessary.

5 Repeat the rolling, dotting, folding and turning twice more, then put the dough in an oiled polythene bag and leave it to rest in the fridge for 30 minutes.

6 Roll and fold the dough twice more, without adding any more butter. Roll out the dough to a large oblong no thicker than 5 cm/¼ in and cut into eight equal smaller squares.

7 To make the glaze, beat together the egg yolk, salt and water and brush over the squares.

8 To make the filling, cut the Brie into eight equal pieces and place a piece in the centre of each square. Roll up and place on a greased baking (cookie) sheet. Cover loosely with oiled clingfilm (plastic wrap) and leave in a warm place for about 45 minutes until doubled in size.

9 Meanwhile, preheat the oven to 200°C/400°F/gas 6/fan oven 180°C. Gently brush the rolls with a little more egg glaze, then sprinkle with the herbs.

10 Bake in the oven for about 25 minutes until puffy and golden. Serve warm. Can be frozen.

Chelsea-style buns

*I don't know anyone who can resist these – moist, fruity,
sticky and light – just as any wheat bun would be!
Serve them with morning coffee, mid-afternoon tea
or even cocoa for supper.*

MAKES 9

For the buns:

1 egg

275 ml/9 fl oz/scant 1¼ cups
warm but not hot milk

50 g/2 oz/¼ cup butter or
margarine, melted

350 g/12 oz/3 cups white gluten-
free flour mix (see pages 11
and 12)

A good pinch of salt

15 ml/1 tbsp xanthum gum

90 g/3½ oz/scant ½ cup light
brown sugar

1 sachet of easy-blend dried yeast

Oil for greasing

10 ml/2 tsp ground cinnamon

100 g/4 oz/⅔ cup dried mixed
fruit (fruit cake mix)

For the glaze:

45 ml/3 tbsp clear honey

30 ml/2 tbsp caster (superfine)
sugar

1 To make the buns, beat together the egg and milk, then
   pour into the breadmaker pan.

2 Add 45 ml/3 tbsp of the melted butter or margarine, the
   flour, salt, gum and 40 g/1½ oz/3 tbsp of the sugar.
   Finally, sprinkle the yeast on top.

3 Set the machine to Dough. When the dough has kneaded
   but has not yet started to heat and rise (about 20
   minutes, depending on the model), switch off the
   machine.

4 Turn out the dough on to a sheet of oiled greaseproof
   (waxed) paper. Place another oiled sheet on top, oiled-
   side down, and roll the dough out to a rectangle about
   23 cm/9 in by 30 cm/12 in.

5 Mix the remaining sugar with the cinnamon and mixed
   fruit. Remove the top piece of greaseproof (waxed)
   paper and brush the dough with the remaining melted
   butter or margarine. Sprinkle the fruit mixture over.

6 Roll up the dough using the second piece of greaseproof paper to help. Cut the roll into nine slices with a wet knife. Place the rolls about 5 mm/¼ in apart, cut-sides up, on an oiled baking (cookie) sheet in three rows of three buns to form a square. Cover loosely with oiled clingfilm (plastic wrap) and leave in a warm place for about 45 minutes until doubled in size and the buns are just sitting snugly side by side.

7 Meanwhile, preheat the oven to 200°C/400°F/gas 6/fan oven 180°C. Remove the clingfilm and bake for about 25 minutes until golden and cooked through.

8 When cooked, remove the buns from the oven. Brush with the honey and sprinkle with the caster sugar while still hot. Best eaten warm. Can be frozen.

Hot cross buns

Now here's something you'll have been missing since you went on a gluten-free diet – spicy, fruit buns. You don't have to save them for Easter, because you can simply omit the crosses if you prefer.

MAKES 10

For the buns:

1 egg

275 ml/9 fl oz/scant 1¼ cups warm but not hot milk

50 g/2 oz/¼ cup butter or margarine, melted

350 g/12 oz/3 cups white gluten-free flour mix (see pages 11 and 12)

A good pinch of salt

15 ml/1 tbsp xanthum gum

10 ml/2 tsp gluten-free mixed (apple pie) spice

50 g/2 oz/¼ cup caster (superfine) sugar

1 sachet of easy-blend dried yeast

100 g/4 oz/⅔ cup dried mixed fruit (fruit cake mix)

Oil for greasing

For the crosses:

50 g/2 oz/½ cup potato flour

15 ml/1 tbsp sunflower oil

A little cold water

For the glaze:

45 ml/3 tbsp clear honey

1 To make the buns, beat together the egg and milk, then pour into the breadmaker pan. Add the melted butter or margarine, the flour, salt, gum, spice and sugar. Finally, sprinkle the yeast on top.

2 Set the machine to Dough. Add the fruit after 15 minutes. When the dough has kneaded but has not yet started to heat and rise (about 20 minutes, depending on the model), switch off the machine.

3 Tip the dough out on to an oiled surface. With oiled hands, shape the dough into 10 balls. Place well apart on an oiled baking (cookie) sheet.

4 Cover with oiled clingfilm (plastic wrap) and leave in a warm place for 45 minutes until doubled in size.

5 Meanwhile, preheat the oven to 200°C/400°F/gas 6/fan oven 180°C.

6 To make the crosses, mix the potato flour with the oil and enough water to form a thick paste. Place in a piping (pastry) bag with a small plain tube (tip) or a plastic bag with the corner cut off and pipe a line across the centre of each row of buns, then a second line vertically down the rows to form a cross on each bun.

7 Bake in the oven for about 25 minutes until golden and cooked through.

8 Remove from the oven and brush with the honey while still hot. Serve warm or split and toasted. Can be frozen.

Doughnut trails

If you have ever taken a holiday in Spain and eaten churros – golden, sweet doughnut strips – you can expect a similar result from this delicious recipe. Serve them freshly cooked, as they do in Spain.

MAKES ABOUT 20

350 ml/12 fl oz/1⅓ cups warm but not hot milk

5 ml/1 tsp salt

65 g/2½ oz/scant ⅓ cup caster (superfine) sugar

225 g/8 oz/2 cups white rice flour

10 ml/2 tsp xanthum gum

10 ml/2 tsp easy-blend dried yeast

Oil for deep-frying

5 ml/1 tsp ground cinnamon (optional)

1 Place the milk, salt and 20 ml/1½ tbsp of the sugar in the breadmaker pan. Add the flour and gum. Finally, sprinkle the yeast on top.

2 Set the machine to Dough.

3 When kneaded and proved, heat the oil for deep-frying to 190°C/ 375°F or until a cube of day-old bread (gluten-free of course!) browns in 30 seconds.

4 Either put the dough in a piping (pastry) bag with a large star tube (tip) or in a plastic bag with the corner of the bag snipped off. Pipe the dough into the hot oil, cutting it off at about 7.5 cm/3 in intervals.

5 Fry (sauté) for about 4 minutes or until golden brown and cooked through, turning the pieces over as necessary. Remove with a draining spoon and drain on kitchen paper (paper towels).

6 Place the pieces in a bag with the remaining sugar and the cinnamon, if using. Hold the bag closed and shake it to coat the doughnuts. Serve while very fresh.

Plain breakfast muffins

Make these in advance ready for breakfast, then warm them briefly in the microwave or oven before serving. They are delicious split and spread with butter and jam or honey.

MAKES 10

1 egg

200 ml/7 fl oz/scant 1 cup milk

50 g/2 oz/¼ cup butter or margarine, melted

225 g/8 oz/2 cups white gluten-free flour mix (see pages 11 and 12)

15 ml/1 tbsp gluten-free baking powder

A pinch of salt

15 g/½ oz/1 tbsp caster (superfine) sugar

1 Line 10 sections of a tartlet tin (patty pan) with paper cake cases (cupcake papers).

2 Beat the egg and milk together and pour into the breadmaker pan with the butter or margarine.

3 Add the remaining ingredients.

4 Set the machine to Dough and run for about 10 minutes until a smooth batter is formed. Switch off the machine.

5 Meanwhile, preheat the oven to 200°C/400°F/gas 6/fan oven 180°C.

6 Turn the batter into the prepared tins – each section should be full – and bake in the oven for 15 minutes until risen, pale golden and the centres spring back when lightly pressed. Transfer to a wire rack. Serve warm. Can be frozen.

Blueberry muffins

I love blueberry muffins! You can substitute raisins for the blueberries if you prefer, in which case you might like to add 2.5 ml/½ tsp gluten-free mixed spice as well to give extra flavour.

MAKES 10

1 egg

200 ml/7 fl oz/scant 1 cup milk

10 ml/2 tsp lemon juice

50 g/2oz/¼ cup butter or margarine, melted

2.5 ml/½ tsp vanilla essence (extract)

225 g/8 oz/2 cups white gluten-free flour mix (see pages 11 and 12)

15 ml/1 tbsp gluten-free baking powder

A pinch of salt

50 g/2 oz/¼ cup caster (superfine) sugar

50 g/2 oz/⅓ cup dried blueberries

1   Line 10 sections of a tartlet tin (patty pan) with paper cake cases (cupcake papers).

2   Beat the egg and milk together and pour into the breadmaker with the lemon juice and butter or margarine.

3   Add the remaining ingredients except the blueberries.

4   Set the machine to Dough and run the machine for 5 minutes. Lift the lid, add the blueberries and continue running the machine for a further 5 minutes or until a smooth batter is formed. Switch off the machine.

5   Meanwhile, preheat the oven to 200°C/400°F/gas 6/fan oven 180°C.

6   Turn the batter into the prepared tins – each section should be full – and bake in the oven for 15 minutes until risen, pale golden and the centres spring back when lightly pressed. Transfer to a wire rack. Serve warm. Can be frozen.

Banana rock muffins

These have all the goodness of cereal and fruit but in a finger food. You can reheat them briefly in the microwave or oven before serving if you like to serve them slightly warm – delicious!

MAKES 12

1 egg

90 ml/6 tbsp water

45 ml/3 tbsp sunflower oil

1 ripe banana, mashed

50 g/2 oz/¼ cup caster (superfine) sugar

A good pinch of salt

1.5 ml/¼ tsp ground cinnamon (optional)

100 g/4 oz/1 cup brown rice flour

50 g/2 oz/½ cup baby rice cereal

15 ml/1 tbsp gluten-free baking powder

2 eating (dessert) apples, peeled, cored and finely chopped

1 Line 12 sections of a tartlet tin (pan) with paper cake cases (cupcake papers).

2 Beat together the egg and water, then pour into the breadmaker pan. Add the oil and banana.

3 Add the remaining ingredients except the apples.

4 Set the machine to Dough and run the machine for 5 minutes. Scrape down the sides, add the apple and run the machine for a further 2 minutes until the mixture is thoroughly blended.

5 Meanwhile, preheat the oven to 200°C/400°F/gas 6/fan oven 180°C.

6 Turn the batter into the prepared tins – each section should be full – and bake in the oven for 10–15 minutes until risen, firm and spongy to the touch. Serve warm. Can be frozen.

Chocolate chip muffins

If you don't like nuts or would prefer an even more chocolately version, simply increase the quantity of chocolate chips. I love to serve these warm with a mug of hot chocolate.

MAKES 12

1 egg

90 ml/6 tbsp water

45 ml/3 tbsp sunflower oil

1 ripe banana, mashed

50 g/2 oz/¼ cup caster (superfine) sugar

A good pinch of salt

100 g/4 oz/1 cup white rice flour

50 g/2 oz/½ cup baby rice cereal

15 ml/1 tbsp gluten-free baking powder

50 g/2 oz/½ cup chopped pistachio nuts

40 g/1½ oz/3 tbsp gluten-free chocolate chips

1 Line 12 sections of a tartlet tin (pan) with paper cake cases (cupcake papers).

2 Beat together the egg and water, then pour into the breadmaker pan. Add the oil and banana.

3 Add the remaining ingredients except the nuts and chocolate chips.

4 Set the machine to Dough and run the machine for 5 minutes. Scrape down the sides, add the nuts and chocolate chips and run the machine for another 2 minutes until the mixture is thoroughly blended.

5 Meanwhile, preheat the oven to 200°C/400°F/gas 6/fan oven 180°C.

6 Turn the batter into the prepared tins – each section should be full – and bake in the oven for 10–15 minutes until risen, firm and spongy to the touch. Serve warm or cold. Can be frozen.

English-style crumpets

These aren't as bubbly as wheat crumpets but the texture and flavour are really good. If bubbles don't appear at all when you cook the first four, add 15 ml/1 tbsp more water for the second batch (these flours are so temperamental!).

MAKES 8

400 ml/14 fl oz/1¾ cups milk and water mixed

15 ml/1 tbsp sunflower oil, plus extra for greasing

2.5 ml/½ tsp salt

20 ml/1½ tbsp caster (superfine) sugar

225 g/8 oz/2 cups white gluten-free flour mix (see pages 11 and 12)

15 ml/1 tbsp xanthum gum

10 ml/2 tsp easy-blend dried yeast

4 ml/¾ tsp bicarbonate of soda (baking soda)

150 ml/¼ pt/⅔ cup warm water

1 Put the milk and water , oil, salt and sugar in the breadmaker pan.

2 Add the flour, gum and lastly the yeast.

3 Set the machine to Dough.

4 When kneaded and proved, remove the pan from the breadmaker and take out the paddle.

5 Mix the bicarbonate of soda with the warm water and mix into the batter with a wooden spoon.

6 Heat a heavy-based frying pan (skillet). Oil four egg rings and place in the pan. Turn down the heat to low.

7 Spoon half the mixture into the four rings. Cook very gently for 25–30 minutes or until set and some bubbles have appeared and burst on the surface (see above).

8 Carefully remove the rings and turn the crumpets over. Cook for 5 minutes only on the other side. Remove from the pan and keep warm in a cloth while cooking the remainder. These are best eaten warm, but they can be toasted later or frozen for future use.

Bagels

Bagels are useful vehicles for all sorts of savoury and sweet fillings or toppings. Don't overcook them or they have a tendency to become hard. If this should happen, split and toast them and eat them whilst still warm.

MAKES 9

1 egg

250 ml/8 fl oz/1 cup warm but not hot water

400 g/14 oz/3½ cups white gluten-free flour mix (see pages 11 and 12), plus extra for dusting

4 ml/¾ tsp salt

10 ml/2 tsp caster (superfine) sugar

1 sachet of easy-blend dried yeast

1 egg yolk

30 ml/2 tbsp water

1 Beat together the egg and water, then pour into the breadmaker pan.

2 Add the flour, salt and sugar, then sprinkle the yeast on top.

3 Set the machine to Dough. When the dough has kneaded but has not yet started to heat and rise (about 20 minutes, depending on the model), switch off the machine and turn the dough out of the pan.

4 With hands dusted in flour, roll the dough into nine balls, then push a finger through the centre to shape into rings.

5 Place on a floured baking (cookie) sheet. Cover loosely with oiled clingfilm (plastic wrap) and leave to rise in a warm place for about 1 hour until doubled in size.

6 Bring a large pan of water to the boil. Using a fish slice, lower in three bagels at a time and boil for 5 minutes, turning over once. Remove from the pan with a draining spoon and place on an oiled baking sheet.

7 Preheat the oven to 200°C/400°F/gas 6/fan oven 180°C.

8 Beat the egg yolk with the water and brush over the bagels.

9 Bake in the oven for about 30 minutes until golden, brushing twice more with the egg glaze during cooking. Transfer to a wire rack and cover with a damp cloth to keep the crusts soft.

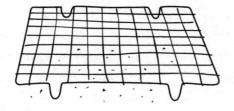

Cakes

～

For all these recipes, I have mixed the ingredients by hand, then cooked them in the breadmaker. Some machines have a cake-making facility but I have found the results variable.

If your cake isn't quite cooked after the chosen amount of time, cook it in further 3-minute bursts so you take care not to overcook it. Some machines can only be set to 1 hour of baking. If so, for some recipes, immediately re-set the timer and continue for the given cooking time.

Most manufacturers recommend lining the pan with non-stick baking parchment for cakes but I found it made little difference, so it's up to you.

You can, of course, use all these recipes and bake them in ordinary cake tins in the oven. I suggest a temperature of 180°C/350°F/ gas 4/fan oven 160°C but you may need to experiment a little.

Simple fruit cake

This is a great storecupboard cake as you can make it with items you are likely to have in your kitchen. If you prefer, you can use all raisins or sultanas (golden raisins) instead of the dried mixed fruit.

MAKES 1 MEDIUM CAKE

175 g/6 oz/³⁄₄ cup light brown sugar

175 g/6 oz/³⁄₄ cup softened butter or soft tub margarine

3 eggs

15 ml/1 tbsp lemon juice

15 ml/1 tbsp milk

100 g/4 oz/²⁄₃ cup dried mixed fruit (fruit cake mix)

225 g/8 oz/2 cups white or brown gluten-free flour mix (see pages 11 and 12)

15 ml/1 tbsp gluten-free baking powder

2.5 ml/¹⁄₂ tsp gluten-free mixed (apple pie) spice

1 Beat the sugar and butter or margarine until light and fluffy. Beat in the eggs one at a time, then add the lemon juice, milk and fruit.

2 Sift together the flour, baking powder and spice. Tip over the surface of the fruit mixture and mix in gently.

3 Remove the paddle from the breadmaker pan. Line the base and sides of the pan with non-stick baking parchment. Add the fruit mixture and level the surface.

4 Set the machine to Bake Only or Extra Bake. Bake for about 1¹⁄₄ hours or until a skewer inserted in the centre comes out clean.

5 Switch off the machine and remove the pan from the breadmaker. Leave the cake in the pan to cool slightly, then turn out on to a wire rack, remove the paper and leave to cool completely. Store in an airtight container.

Giant chocolate cupcake

*This has the classic texture of little cup cakes
– a rich crumbly cake with a thick layer of sweet
chocolate icing. It's great for birthday teas
and special occasions.*

MAKES 1 MEDIUM CAKE

100 g/4 oz/½ cup soft tub margarine

100 g/4 oz/½ cup light brown sugar

2 eggs, beaten

125 g/4½ oz/generous 1 cup white gluten-free flour mix (see pages 11 and 12)

10 ml/2 tsp gluten-free baking powder

50 g/2 oz/½ cup gluten-free cocoa (unsweetened chocolate) powder

75 ml/5 tbsp water

225 g/8 oz/1⅓ cups icing (confectioners') sugar

1 Beat together the margarine and sugar in a bowl until light and fluffy. Beat in the eggs.

2 Sift the flour, baking powder and half the cocoa powder into a second bowl.

3 Tip the flour mixture into the egg mixture and fold in with a metal spoon, adding 30 ml/2 tbsp of the water. The mixture should have a very soft dropping consistency, if not add a little more water.

4 Remove the paddle from the breadmaker pan. Line the base and sides of the pan with non-stick baking parchment and tip in the mixture.

5 Set the machine to Bake Only or Extra Bake. Bake for 50 minutes until risen and the centre springs back when lightly pressed.

6 Switch off the machine and remove the pan from the breadmaker. Leave the cake in the pan for 10 minutes, then turn out on to a wire rack, remove the paper and leave to cool completely.

7 Sift the icing sugar with the remaining cocoa powder. Mix with 45 ml/3 tbsp water to form a thick, creamy icing (frosting). Spread over the top of the cooled cake and leave to set. Store in an airtight container.

Chocolate block cake

This is an even more seriously chocolatey cake than the Giant Chocolate Cupcake on page 132! It has a slightly moister texture as well as a pure chocolate top.

MAKES 1 MEDIUM CAKE

175 g/6 oz/³/₄ cup granulated sugar

175 g/6 oz/³/₄ cup butter or margarine

45 ml/3 tbsp warm water

3 eggs, beaten

5 ml/1 tsp vanilla essence (extract)

175 g/6 oz/1¹/₂ cup white gluten-free flour mix (see pages 11 and 12)

60 ml/4 tbsp gluten-free cocoa (unsweetened chocolate) powder

15 ml/1 tbsp gluten-free baking powder

1.5 ml/¹/₄ tsp salt

100 g/4 oz/1 cup gluten-free plain (semi-sweet) chocolate, broken into pieces

1 Put the sugar and butter or margarine in a saucepan with the water and heat until melted. Beat in the eggs and vanilla.

2 Sift the flour, cocoa powder, baking powder and salt into a bowl. Pour in the melted mixture and mix well.

3 Remove the paddle from the breadmaker pan. Line the base and sides of the pan with non-stick baking parchment and tip in the mixture.

4 Set the machine to Bake Only or Extra Bake. Bake for about 1 hour or until firm to the touch, taking care not to over-cook or the cake will become too dry.

5 Switch off the machine and remove the pan from the breadmaker. Leave the cake in the pan for 10 minutes, then turn out on to a wire rack, remove the paper and leave to cool completely.

6 Melt the chocolate in a bowl over a pan of hot water or briefly in the microwave. Spread over the top of the cake and leave to set. Store in an airtight container.

Jammy vanilla cake

This is a good cake for everyday eating. You can also try filling it with fresh crushed strawberries or raspberries and a layer of whipped cream to create a delicious dessert worthy of a special lunch or dinner.

MAKES 1 MEDIUM CAKE

175 g/6 oz/³⁄₄ cup caster (superfine) sugar, plus extra for sprinkling

5 ml/1 tsp vanilla essence (extract)

175 g/6 oz/³⁄₄ cup softened butter or soft tub margarine

3 eggs

225 g/8 oz/2 cups white gluten-free flour mix (see pages 11 and 12)

10 ml/2 tsp gluten-free baking powder

30 ml/2 tbsp milk

60 ml/4 tbsp raspberry jam (conserve)

A little sifted icing (confectioners') sugar for dusting

1 Beat the sugar, vanilla and butter or margarine until light and fluffy. Beat in the eggs one at a time.

2 Sift together the flour and baking powder, then tip over the surface of the egg mixture and fold in with a metal spoon. Add enough of the milk to form a soft dropping consistency.

3 Remove the paddle from the breadmaker pan. Line the base and sides of the pan with non-stick baking parchment and tip in the mixture.

4 Set the machine to Bake Only or Extra Bake. Cook for about 1¼ hours until golden and firm to the touch.

5 Switch off the machine and remove the pan from the breadmaker. Leave the cake in the pan for 10 minutes, then turn out on to a wire rack, remove the paper and leave to cool completely.

6 Split the cake in half horizontally, then sandwich together with the jam. Dust the top of the cake with sifted icing sugar. Store in an airtight container.

Sultana almond cake

Another great version of this recipe is to omit the sultanas and use chopped pistachio nuts instead of almonds, and almond essence instead of the cinnamon.

MAKES 1 MEDIUM CAKE

175 g/6 oz/³/₄ cup light brown sugar

175 g/6 oz/³/₄ cup softened butter or soft tub margarine

3 eggs

15 ml/1 tbsp lemon juice

15 ml/1 tbsp milk

100 g/4 oz/²/₃ cup sultanas (golden raisins)

50 g/2 oz/¹/₂ cup flaked (slivered) almonds

225 g/8 oz/2 cups white or brown gluten-free flour mix (see pages 11 and 12)

10 ml/2 tsp gluten-free baking powder

2.5 ml/¹/₂ tsp ground cinnamon

8 whole blanched almonds

1 Beat the sugar and butter or margarine until light and fluffy. Beat in the eggs one at a time, then add the lemon juice, milk, sultanas and flaked almonds.

2 Sift together the flour, baking powder and cinnamon. Tip over the surface of the fruit mixture and mix in gently.

3 Remove the paddle from the breadmaker pan. Line the base and sides of the pan with non-stick baking parchment. Add the fruit mixture and level the surface.

4 Set the machine to Bake Only or Extra Bake. Bake for 45 minutes, then quickly open the lid as little as possible and arrange the whole almonds on top. Close the lid gently.

5 Cook for a further 30 minutes or until the cake is golden and firm and skewer inserted in the centre comes out clean.

6 Switch off the machine and remove the pan from the breadmaker. Leave the cake in the pan for 10 minutes, then turn out on to a wire rack, remove the paper and leave to cool completely. Store in an airtight container.

Date and walnut cake

A favourite combination of textures and flavours, this moist cake is a delicious teatime treat. Try making it with chopped ready-to-eat dried apricots and almonds instead of the dates and walnuts.

MAKES 1 MEDIUM CAKE

50 g/2 oz/¹/₃ cup chopped cooking dates

50 g/2 oz/¹/₄ cup glacé (candied) cherries, chopped

50 g/2 oz/¹/₃ cup sultanas (golden raisins)

50 g/2 oz/¹/₂ cup chopped walnuts

200 ml/7 fl oz/scant 1 cup orange juice

150 g/5 oz/²/₃ cup soft tub margarine

30 ml/2 tbsp black cherry jam (conserve)

100 g/4 oz/¹/₂ cup light brown sugar

2 eggs, beaten

225 g/8 oz/2 cups white gluten-free flour mix (see pages 11 and 12)

10 ml/2 tsp gluten-free baking powder

4 glacé cherries, halved, for decoration

1 Put the fruits and nuts in a pan. Add the orange juice and bring to the boil. Leave to cool.

2 Beat the margarine, jam and sugar together until light and fluffy. Beat in the eggs, then stir in the fruit and nuts. Mix together the flour and baking powder and mix in.

3 Remove the paddle from the breadmaker pan. Line the base and sides of the pan with non-stick baking parchment. Gently turn the mixture into the lined pan.

4 Set the machine to Bake Only or Extra Bake. Bake for 1 hour, then gently open the lid as little as possible and arrange the halved cherries over the surface. Gently shut the lid and bake for a further 30 minutes until a skewer inserted in the centre comes out clean.

5 Switch off the machine and remove the pan from the breadmaker. Leave the cake in the pan for 10 minutes, then turn out on to a wire rack, remove the paper and leave to cool completely. Store in an airtight container.

Apple and fruit cake

The apple really does make this cake deliciously moist.
The pectin in the skin of the fruit helps give it a lovely
sponginess too, so you can be sure
of an excellent result.

MAKES 1 MEDIUM CAKE

175 g/6 oz/¾ cup softened
butter or soft tub margarine

175 g/6 oz/¾ cup caster
(superfine) sugar

3 large eggs

2 eating (dessert) apples, grated,
including the skin

225 g/8 oz/1⅓ cups dried mixed
fruit (fruit cake mix)

120 ml/4 fl oz/½ cup apple juice

100 g/4 oz/½ cup brown rice
flour

150 g/5 oz/1¼ cups soya flour

15 ml/1 tbsp gluten-free baking
powder

2.5 ml/½ tsp ground cloves

1 Beat together the butter or margarine and sugar until
light and fluffy. Beat in the eggs, one at a time, then beat
in the apples and dried fruit. Stir in the apple juice.

2 Sift together all the remaining ingredients, then fold into
the apple mixture with a metal spoon.

3 Remove the paddle from the breadmaker pan. Line the
base and sides of the pan with non-stick baking
parchment. Spoon in the mixture and level the surface.

4 Set the machine to Bake Only or Extra Bake. Bake for
about 1½ hours until firm and a skewer inserted in the
centre comes out clean.

5 Switch off the machine and remove the pan from the
breadmaker. Leave the cake in the pan for 10 minutes,
then turn out on to a wire rack, remove the paper and
leave to cool completely. Store in an airtight container.

Coconut cake

A plain cake that's delicious on its own or you can brush the surface with warm raspberry jam and coat it in more desiccated coconut for a very special finish.

MAKES 1 MEDIUM CAKE

175 g/6 oz/³/₄ cup caster (superfine) sugar, plus extra for sprinkling

5 ml/1 tsp vanilla essence (extract)

175 g/6 oz/³/₄ cup softened butter or soft tub margarine

3 eggs

225 g/8 oz/2 cups white gluten-free flour mix (see pages 11 and 12)

10 ml/2 tsp gluten-free baking powder

75 g/3 oz/³/₄ cup desiccated (shredded) coconut

30 ml/2 tbsp milk

1 Using an electric beater, beat the sugar, vanilla and butter or margarine until light and fluffy. Beat in the eggs one at a time.

2 Sift together the flour and baking powder. Tip over the surface of the cake mixture and add the coconut. Mix in gently. Add enough of the milk to form a soft dropping consistency.

3 Remove the paddle from the breadmaker pan. Line the base and sides of the pan with non-stick baking parchment. Gently turn the mixture into the lined pan.

4 Set the machine to Bake Only or Extra Bake. Bake for 1¼ hours or until risen and firm to the touch.

5 Switch off the machine and remove the pan from the breadmaker. Leave the cake in the pan for 10 minutes, then turn out on to a wire rack, remove the paper and leave to cool completely. Sprinkle with a little caster sugar. Store in an airtight container.

Tropicana cake

A nutritious cake with lots of flavour and a delicious moistness. Try it with lime marmalade for a hint of added zest. You can also make it with ordinary dried mixed fruit if you prefer.

MAKES 1 MEDIUM CAKE

225 g/8 oz/1⅓ cups dried fruit salad

200 ml/7 fl oz/scant 1 cup boiling water

150 g/5 oz/⅔ cup soft tub margarine

30 ml/2 tbsp orange marmalade

100 g/4 oz/½ cup light brown sugar

2 eggs, beaten

225 g/8 oz/2 cups brown gluten-free flour mix (see pages 11 and 12)

10 ml/2 tsp gluten-free baking powder

5 ml/1 tsp ground cinnamon

15 ml/1 tbsp demerara sugar

1 Chop the dried fruit, discarding any stones (pits). Place in a bowl and cover with the boiling water. Leave to soak for several hours or preferably overnight.

2 Beat the margarine, marmalade and sugar together until light and fluffy. Beat in the eggs, then stir in the fruit.

3 Mix together the flour, baking powder and cinnamon. Add to the fruit mixture and mix gently but thoroughly.

4 Remove the paddle from the breadmaker pan. Line the base and sides of the pan with non-stick baking parchment. Gently turn the mixture into the lined pan and sprinkle with the demerara sugar.

5 Set the machine to Bake Only or Extra Bake. Bake for about 1½ hours or until risen and firm to the touch.

6 Switch off the machine and remove the pan from the breadmaker. Leave the cake in the pan for 10 minutes, then turn out on to a wire rack, remove the paper and leave to cool completely. Store in an airtight container.

Seed cake

This is an old-fashioned cake, plain but with a hint of aniseed flavour. It is particularly good served mid-morning with coffee. This cake really does need to be made with butter to give the right flavour.

MAKES 1 MEDIUM CAKE

175 g/6 oz/³/₄ cup softened butter

175 g/6 oz/³/₄ cup caster (superfine) sugar

3 eggs

15 ml/1 tbsp caraway seeds

225 g/8 oz/2 cups white gluten-free flour mix (see pages 11 and 12)

10 ml/2 tsp gluten-free baking powder

10 ml/2 tsp xanthum gum

1 Beat the butter and sugar until light and fluffy. Beat in the eggs one at a time. Stir in the caraway seeds.

2 Sift together the flour, baking powder and gum. Sprinkle over the surface of the egg mixture and fold in gently with a metal spoon.

3 Remove the paddle from the breadmaker pan. Line the base and sides of the pan with non-stick baking parchment and gently turn the mixture into the lined pan. Level the surface.

4 Set the machine to Bake Only or Extra Bake. Bake for 1 hour or until risen and firm to the touch.

5 Switch off the machine and remove the pan from the breadmaker. Leave the cake in the pan for 10 minutes, then turn out on to a wire rack, remove the paper and leave to cool. Store in an airtight container.

Parkin

You can experiment with buckwheat or quinoa grains instead of millet if you prefer. For a plain gingerbread simply omit the grains altogether and do not ice it.

MAKES 1 MEDIUM CAKE

For the cake:

50 g/2 oz/½ cup millet grains

150 ml/¼ pt/⅔ cup milk

50 g/2 oz/¼ cup butter or margarine

75 ml/5 tbsp black treacle (molasses)

75 ml/5 tbsp golden (light corn) syrup

5 ml/1 tsp bicarbonate of soda (baking soda)

1 large egg, beaten

225 g/8 oz/2 cups brown gluten-free flour mix (see pages 11 and 12)

15 ml/1 tbsp gluten-free baking powder

5 ml/1 tsp ground ginger

For the icing (frosting):

100 g/4 oz/⅔ cup icing (confectioners') sugar, sifted

20 ml/1½ tbsp water or lemon juice

1 Put the millet, milk, butter or margarine, treacle and syrup in a saucepan and heat, stirring, until the fat melts. Leave to cool for 5 minutes.

2 Stir in the bicarbonate of soda and beat in the egg.

3 Sift together the flour, baking powder and ginger and fold into the melted mixture.

4 Remove the paddle from the breadmaker pan. Line the base and sides of the pan with non-stick baking parchment. Tip the mixture into the lined pan and level the surface.

5 Set the machine to Bake Only or Extra Bake. Bake for 1 hour or until firm and a skewer inserted in the centre comes out clean.

6 Switch off the machine and remove the pan from the breadmaker. Leave the cake in the pan for 10 minutes to cool slightly. Turn out on to a wire rack, remove the paper and leave to cool completely.

7 Mix the icing sugar with the water or lemon juice to form a thick cream. Spread over the top of the cake and leave to set. Store in an airtight container.

Mocha marble cake

Marble cakes always look very effective when cut and, as these cakes are all made in the breadmaker pan, they are best served already sliced and arranged on a plate, as the shape isn't that inspiring as a whole!

MAKES 1 MEDIUM CAKE

175 g/6 oz/³/₄ cup caster (superfine) sugar

175 g/6 oz/³/₄ cup softened butter or soft tub margarine

3 eggs

225 g/8 oz/2 cups white gluten-free flour mix (see pages 11 and 12)

10 ml/2 tsp gluten-free baking powder

A pinch of salt

30 ml/2 tbsp gluten-free cocoa (unsweetened chocolate) powder

60 ml/4 tbsp warm water

5ml/1 tsp instant coffee granules

2.5 ml/¹/₂ tsp vanilla essence (extract)

1 Beat together the sugar and butter or margarine until light and fluffy. Beat in the eggs one at a time.

2 Sift together the flour, baking powder and salt. Tip over the surface of the egg mixture and fold in with a metal spoon. Divide the mixture into three equal portions.

3 Blend the cocoa with 30 ml/2 tbsp of the water and fold into one portion.

4 Blend the coffee with half the remaining water and fold into the second portion.

5 Blend the vanilla into the third portion with the remaining water.

6 Remove the paddle from the breadmaker pan. Line the base and sides of the pan with non-stick baking parchment. Put alternate spoonfuls of the three mixtures in the pan, then lightly swirl them so they blend a bit but leave a marbled effect.

7 Set the machine to Bake Only or Extra Bake. Cook for about 1¼ hours until firm to the touch and a skewer inserted in the centre comes out clean.

8 Switch off the machine and remove the pan from the breadmaker. Leave the cake in the pan for 10 minutes, then turn out on to a wire rack, remove the paper and leave to cool completely. Store in an airtight container.

Iced orange slice

Orange cakes are always popular. This one has a nice open texture and a tangy orange icing. For children you could add a few drops of orange food colouring to the icing if you like.

MAKES 1 MEDIUM CAKE

For the cake:

175 g/6 oz/¾ cup softened butter or soft tub margarine

175 g/6 oz/¾ cup light brown sugar

Finely grated zest and juice of 1 large orange

3 eggs

225 g/8 oz/2 cups white gluten-free flour mix (see pages 11 and 12)

10 ml/2 tsp gluten-free baking powder

For the icing (frosting):

100 g/4 oz/⅔ cup softened butter

225 g/8 oz/1⅓ cups icing (confectioners') sugar, sifted

Orange jelly slices to decorate

1 To make the cake, beat together the butter or margarine, sugar and half the orange zest until light and fluffy. Beat in the eggs one at a time.

2 Sift together the flour and baking powder. Sprinkle over the surface of the egg mixture and fold in gently with a metal spoon. Add 30 ml/2 tbsp of the orange juice to form a soft, dropping consistency.

3 Remove the paddle from the breadmaker pan. Line the base and sides of the pan with non-stick baking parchment and gently turn the mixture into the lined pan. Level the surface.

4 Set the machine to Bake Only or Extra Bake. Bake for about 1¼ hours until risen and firm to the touch.

5 Switch off the machine and remove the pan from the breadmaker. Leave the cake in the pan for 10 minutes, then turn out on to a wire rack, remove the paper and leave to cool completely.

6 To make the icing, beat the butter with the icing sugar until smooth. Beat in the remaining orange zest and any remaining juice to form a spreadable icing. If necessary, add a little more icing sugar.

7 Split the cake in half. Sandwich together with half the icing, then spread the remainder over the surface. Decorate with orange jelly slices and leave to set. Store in an airtight container.

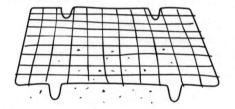

Lime drizzle cake

You can use the grated zest and half the juice of a lemon instead of the limes, if you prefer, to make a traditional lemon drizzle cake, although the lime makes it more unusual.

MAKES 1 MEDIUM CAKE

For the cake:

175 g/6 oz/³/₄ cup softened butter or soft tub margarine

175 g/6 oz/³/₄ cup caster (superfine) sugar

Finely grated zest of 1 lime

3 eggs

225 g/8 oz/2 cups white gluten-free flour mix (see pages 11 and 12)

10 ml/2 tsp gluten-free baking powder

For the icing (frosting):

Thinly pared zest and juice of 1 lime

100 g/4 oz/¹/₂ cup caster (superfine) sugar

1 To make the cake, beat together the butter or margarine, sugar and lime zest until light and fluffy. Beat in the eggs one at a time.

2 Sift together the flour and baking powder. Sprinkle over the surface of the egg mixture and fold in gently with a metal spoon.

3 Remove the paddle from the breadmaker. Line the base and sides of the pan with non-stick baking parchment and turn the mixture into the pan. Level the surface.

4 Set the machine to Bake Only or Extra Bake. Bake for about 1¹/₄ hours or until risen and firm to the touch.

5 Switch off the machine and remove the pan from the breadmaker. Leave the cake in the pan for 10 minutes, then turn out on to a wire rack and remove the paper.

6 To make the icing, thinly shred the lime zest and boil in water for 2 minutes. Drain, rinse with cold water and drain again. Mix together with the sugar and lime juice. Spoon over the surface of the cake and leave to cool completely. Store in an airtight container.

Carrot cake

Everyone loves carrot cake and even though this has no wheat flour in it, the texture is moist and delicious. You can ice it (see Frosted Carrot Cake on page 150) and try flavouring the topping with orange instead of lemon.

MAKES 1 MEDIUM CAKE

150 ml/¼ pt/⅔ cup milk

75 g/3 oz/⅓ cup butter or margarine

40 g/1½ oz/3 tbsp caster (superfine) sugar

175 g/6 oz/½ cup golden (light corn) syrup

5 ml/1 tsp bicarbonate of soda (baking soda)

1 large egg, beaten

2 large carrots, grated

275 g/10 oz/2½ cups white gluten-free flour mix (see pages 11 and 12)

15 ml/1 tbsp gluten-free baking powder

5 ml/1 tsp ground cinnamon

1 Put the milk, butter or margarine, sugar and syrup in a pan and heat gently until the fat melts. Leave to cool for 5 minutes.

2 Stir in the bicarbonate of soda, egg and carrots.

3 Sift together the remaining ingredients and fold into the mixture with a metal spoon.

4 Remove the paddle from the breadmaker pan. Line the base and sides of the pan with non-stick baking parchment and gently turn the mixture into the lined pan. Level the surface.

5 Set the machine to Bake Only or Extra Bake. Bake for about 1 hour or until risen and firm to the touch.

6 Switch off the machine and remove the pan from the breadmaker. Leave the cake in the pan for 10 minutes, then turn out on to a wire rack, remove the paper and leave to cool. Store in an airtight container.

Frosted carrot cake

This is a grander version of the Carrot Cake on page 149, lovely to impress friends who pop round for coffee or a cup of tea. They'll never know it's made with your 'funny' flour! They might even ask for the recipe.

MAKES 1 MEDIUM CAKE

For the cake:

150 ml/¹/₄ pt/²/₃ cup milk

50 g/2 oz/¹/₄ cup butter or margarine

40 g/1¹/₂ oz/3 tbsp caster (superfine) sugar

175 g/6 oz/¹/₂ cup golden (light corn) syrup

5 ml/1 tsp bicarbonate of soda (baking soda)

1 large egg, beaten

2 large carrots, grated

75 g/3 oz/³/₄ cup chopped walnuts

225 g/8 oz/2 cups white gluten-free flour mix (see pages 11 and 12)

15 ml/1 tbsp gluten-free baking powder

5 ml/1 tsp ground cinnamon

For the frosting:

50 g/2 oz/¹/₄ cup softened butter

175 g/6 oz/1 cup of icing (confectioners') sugar, sifted

Finely grated zest and juice of ¹/₂ lemon

A few walnut halves to decorate

1 To make the cake, put the milk, butter or margarine, sugar and syrup in a pan and heat gently until the fat melts. Leave to cool for 5 minutes.

2 Stir in the bicarbonate of soda, the egg and carrots.

3 Sift together the remaining ingredients and fold into the mixture with a metal spoon.

4 Remove the paddle from the breadmaker pan. Line the base and sides of the pan with non-stick baking parchment and gently turn the mixture into the lined pan. Level the surface.

5 Set the machine to Bake Only or Extra Bake. Bake for about 1 hour or until risen and firm to the touch.

6 Switch off the machine and remove the pan from the breadmaker. Leave the cake in the pan for 10 minutes, then turn out on to a wire rack, remove the paper and leave to cool.

7 To make the frosting, beat the butter in a bowl until very soft, then work in the icing sugar, lemon zest and enough of the lemon juice to form a soft icing that still holds its shape.

8 Spread the frosting over the cold cake and decorate with the walnut halves. Store in an airtight container.

Useful Addresses

Ingredients by mail order

Many of the products used in this book can be bought from your local health food shop but some, such as tapioca flour, are not so readily available. Everything, however, can be bought by mail order and it's a convenient and sometimes cheaper way to shop. I do all my shopping online, but you can, of course, phone or write to them for a catalogue instead.

GoodnessDirect
South March
Daventry
Northamptonshire NN11 4PH
Telephone: 01327 301135
Website: www.goodnessdirect.co.uk

Innovative Solutions UK Limited
Tunstall Road
Bosley
Nr Macclesfield
Cheshire SK11 0PE
Telephone: 0845 6013151
Website: www.innovative-solutions.org.uk

Some of the major supermarkets also offer online shopping, so you can look at their websites for information on the gluten-free products they stock.

Asda
Telephone: 0500 100055
Website: www.asda.co.uk

Sainsbury's
Telephone: 0845 301 2020
Website: www.sainsburys.co.uk

Tesco
Telephone: 0800 505 555
Website: www.tesco.com

Waitrose
Telephone: 01344 825235
Website: www.waitrose.com

Information and support services

Action Against Allergy
PO Box 278
Twickenham
Middlesex TW1 4QQ
Telephone: 020 8892 2711
E-mail: AAA@actionagainstallergy.freeserve.co.uk
Website: www.actionagainstallergy.co.uk
(Please enclose an sae when writing to the society for information)

The British Allergy Foundation
Deepdene House
30 Bellgrove Road
Welling
Kent DA16 3PY
Helpline: 020 8303 8583
Website: www.allergyfoundation.com

The Coeliac Society
PO Box 220
High Wycombe
Buckinghamshire HP11 2HY
Telephone: 01494 437278
Website: www.coeliac.co.uk

The National Society for Research into Allergy
PO Box 45
Hinckley
Leicestershire LE10 1JY
Telephone: 01455 250715
Website: www.all-allergy.co.uk

Index